MAMAN
مامان

MAMAN
مامان

The Life Story of an Iranian-Jewish Mother

Moris K. Niknam

Book Design & Production
Columbus Publishing Lab
www.ColumbusPublishingLab.com

Copyright © 2016 by Moris Niknam
LCCN 2016946607

All rights reserved. This book, or parts thereof, may not be reproduced in any form without permission.

Paperback ISBN 978-1-63337-109-5
E-book ISBN 978-1-63337-111-8

Printed in the United States of America
1 3 5 7 9 10 8 6 4 2

*To my sister Lili, who never left Maman's side
and took care of her with all her strength and soul.*

*To my father, Baba Nourie, who stayed with
and supported Maman throughout their years together.*

*To my wife for her prayers, support,
and encouragement to finish this book.*

CHAPTER ONE

NANA—A WOMAN OF FAITH AND STRENGTH

THE YEAR WAS 1932. The place was Tehran, the capital of Iran. The entire country was facing two major disasters: economic and political instabilities. Even though Iran was the second largest oil export in the world, there was always struggle to balance the political powers and the economic situation. Despite the uncertainties of the future of Iran, there was an unbreakable motivation amongst the Iranian families, a rich culture where the love of family and traditions were the center of their lives. This culture has been cultivated in the heart of the Iranian families since the beginning of their country's history. Even though Iran has always been an Islamic country populated by a majority of Shia

Muslims, there were hundreds or thousands of non-Muslim Iranians such as Zoroastrians, Baha'is, Christians, and Jews, who lived in various parts of the country for centuries.

An old mud-structured housing community of several poor neighborhoods stood in a remote region in northern Tehran. This shantytown housed several Iranian Jewish and Muslim families.

Nana, a short, barely five-feet tall, eighteen-year-old devoted Jewish woman, lived in a one-story house with her young husband, Rahim. He was rarely home and was usually searching for odd jobs in order to take care of his young wife. There was virtually no economy in Iran. The pain of poverty infected everyone—Jews and non-Jews alike. With their tiny income and a few household treasures such as a pot and a ladle, Nana was able to prepare a small meal or two each day along with performing many cleaning chores in between. She was a strong-willed woman with two perfect priorities in her life: God and family. Her faith in God and attention to the Jewish traditions, especially the Sabbath, the holiest day in Judaism, gave her the strength to move on each day.

Nana was used to pain and mental anguish, especially being rejected and looked down upon by many hateful fanatical Muslim neighbors each time she left her house. But it did not bother her much since she found several passionate Muslim mothers who cared more about taking care of their poor family members than focusing on a wasteful hatred toward non-Muslims.

"Thank God for these people," Nana repeated daily. She often wondered why King Cyrus, whom she had heard about from readings of the Jewish Torah (Ezra 4:16), kept the Jews in Persia (Iran) amongst a large non-Jewish population. *What if the Jews had all moved to another more hospitable land? Wouldn't there then be less hate and animosity toward Jews?* Nana wondered. Nevertheless, Nana believed the life they lived was God's plan, so she smiled to herself, being satisfied in God's words.

Nana was blessed with visits from distant relatives living nearby who often stopped over to see if she was doing well and to check to make sure she had prepared delicious Persian stews such as Ab-Goosht or the main dish of Khoreshteh Karafs, for which she was famous. She regularly asked her women relatives to stay for the Sabbath to light the candles together. She needed the extra support, and not having her husband around much, she wanted to share her faith and the

Sabbath prayers with her relatives. These special times each week gave Nana the strength to move forward. This day, she needed a little more strength and support. She was pregnant.

CHAPTER TWO

BIRTH AND YOUNG LIFE OF AZIZA—OUR MAMAN

IT WAS A DARK, COLD NIGHT. Nana started to feel the labor pains coming more and more often. Her husband was away for several days, so she prayed to God constantly, asking to have her relatives stop by. There were no phones or other means of communication, and no doctor or midwife. She managed to step out of the house while panting from the pains and move to a nearby house to alert her trusted Muslim mother, Zahra. Nana was happy to see that Zahra was awake and willing to go out of her way to alert Nana's relatives.

"Just ask for Monire to come," Nana told Zahra. "She is the closest relative who knows how to help me with pregnancy," Nana continued.

Zahra agreed and helped Nana go back to her room to relax.

"Don't worry, Nana," Zahra said in a caring voice, "Negaran Nabash, Allah-o-Akbar [meaning: don't worry, God is Great]."

Within less than half an hour, Monire came into the room with Zahra.

"You don't have to be here, my dear neighbor Zahra. Monire will take care of me," Nana said with a thankful gesture.

The labor pains became more intense. Monire asked Nana to take her tight clothes off to prepare for the birth of her first child. She started to squat by a force of nature, hoping to see her child drop down on an old worn-out Persian carpet soon. But it did not happen that night.

It was almost dawn and Nana was still struggling to push her baby out. Monire was a great help to Nana, providing clean water and washcloths to soothe Nana's pain.

All of a sudden, there were knocks on the door, and the sound of voices getting louder and louder.

"Oh…no, not now," Nana said in pain. "These stupid Muslim kids often come and tease me by knocking on my door early in the mornings."

The voices were heard saying: "You old Joohood [filthy Jew] woman." The boys repeated this for some time and then disappeared.

Nana was used to this hassle and normally wasn't bothered by it at all, but this time she was slightly angry. Perhaps the mild anger gave her more energy to push. Monire could see some thick black hair and soon a head and finally the full body of a beautiful baby girl.

"Khodar-Ra-Shokr [Thank God]," both Nana and Monire repeated together with happiness and relief.

This reddish-black-haired, brown-eyed baby was born to be our future mother (**Maman**), whose full name was Khanom-Agha Aziza Davood-Esfahani Niknam. Now holding Aziza in her weak arms, Nana asked Monire to help her get up and start planning the day's next meal. That was the usual practice then for any Iranian mother.

Monire stayed for a while to clean up after cutting the umbilical cord and making sure the baby was well adjusted to nursing.

"Come back soon, Monire," Nana begged with a big smile on her face.

"Beh Omideh Khoda [God willing], I will come soon,"

Monire replied happily.

Aziza grew up in a very poor environment, in a dirt-poor family, with a father who was hardly around, but she was always safe with Nana. During several years of living in the same house, Nana never lost her faith in God, which gave her the strength needed to raise six more children. Her utmost goal was to show her family that with love of God, everything is possible in life no matter the circumstances.

Nana was an expert in two major tasks: cooking and observing Jewish High Holidays. Even though it took her several hours to cook a Persian meal over a heating tool with three faint flames, the children never complained about having to wait to eat. Celebrating the Jewish Sabbath every Friday evening was the most exciting time for the entire family. The family togetherness with some relatives, lighting the Sabbath candles while reciting Hebrew prayers, meant so much to Nana and were unforgettable memories. Another exciting moment was when each of the children reached age thirteen, which automatically meant the entry into manhood for the boys (Bar Mitzvah) and marriage for the girls—especially for her precious daughter Aziza—according to Jewish marriage customs. Perhaps this was God's design so parents could be spared the painful teenage years. When the time finally arrived, our Maman, age thirteen, was clueless about what would soon happen that would change her life forever.

The Wedding

"Quickly, get ready for your biggest surprise. Hurry up and make yourself beautiful," Nana said excitedly to Aziza. "I have also invited two of your closest girlfriends over," Nana continued.

"Are we going to play a game?" Aziza asked with a puzzled look while straightening her hair with a brush.

"Just wait, my little girl," Nana smiled. "All I can tell you is that you will be full of joy for the rest of your life when you discover your surprise."

Soon Nana heard knocking at the door, but this time instead of voices from the problem kids there was a nonstop silly giggle. When Nana opened the door, she was delighted to see two teenage girls.

"Come in, girls," Nana said to the teens. "Aziza will be here soon. I have to go and prepare the Korsi."

Aziza and the teens, tucked under the Korsi's warm

blankets, were nervous about what to expect. The Korsi, which was the only source of heat in the house, was made of a square-shaped coffee table with a metallic bowl containing hot charcoals placed in the center of the table. Heavy blankets covered the whole table in order to keep the heat contained under the Korsi. There were several heavy pillows around the ends of the blankets where the family members could sit around comfortably with their feet tucked under the blankets to enjoy the warmth of the hot charcoals.

Finally, a seventeen-year-old, tall, handsome young man with shiny black hair, thick eyebrows, and dark Jewish eyes appeared in the room. Apparently, he was Nana's surprise, but she was quiet and anxiously waited for the next move.

The teenage boy smiled. He was "the man in charge" of choosing which young lady under the Korsi was going to be his everlasting wife. He sat on the opposite side of the Korsi facing the girls. He stared at each one, eyes moving from right to left and back again, checking each girl out. When his search was completed, his eyes finally settled on the middle girl—Aziza, our mother, Maman. "Yes, I want that one," he said excitedly. The other girls then looked at Aziza and shrugged their shoulders, as if to say, "*Oh well. I guess we are not the ones to play this game.*"

So the wife had been chosen. No one could oppose it, and nothing could separate the new couple until death do them part. Soon after, the boy Nourie and the girl Aziza were supposed to join together and make the Godly covenant of marriage for the rest of their lives. And this excited young boy was soon going to be our father, Baba Nourie.

Nana informed her relatives of the good news of the marriage agreement and asked for any help they could provide for the ceremony since there was so little money available to cover the cost of the wedding. Even though money was tight, there were always open prayers and time for God to intervene. After all, this was not going to be the first "miracle" that would happen in Maman's life journey. These were God's chosen people who were about to extend the Jewish line from His Iranian Jews who were freed by one of history's greatest kings, Cyrus the Great.

So Nana kept praying in her heart for a decent wedding for her first precious child, and it did not take too long for Nana's prayers to be answered.

Monire found a distant relative whose husband had a business in the heart of Tehran. He was delighted to cover the cost of the wedding dress and a nice suit for the groom, which were very costly at that time. In addition, other family members and a few neighbors agreed to provide delicious Persian food and some flowers—mostly Maman's favorite red roses!

The young bride and groom were delighted to obey the sacred Jewish matrimonial covenant in which the man and the woman become one flesh, according to the first chapter of the Torah (Genesis 2:24), and love one another until death do them part. They looked at each other with sweet smiles while Nana was busy talking to her relatives about the wedding details.

"Do you have a lot of trouble from your neighbors here in Tehran?" Baba Nourie asked while his eyes were fixed on Maman's beautiful reddish-brown hair and his nose was intoxicated by the unknown homemade perfume she was wearing.

"Well…sort of," Maman replied in a shy voice. "Why do you ask now? Is it bad in Esfahan city where you come from?"

"It is worse, but I don't want to talk about it now," Baba Nourie said. Maman noticed a change in Baba Nourie's face and voice. It was an unhappy one, so she changed the subject quickly.

"I have a funny question for you," Maman said. "Why is your name Nourie?" she asked with an intense curiosity. "My mom said your real name is Noor-Allah, right?" she continued.

"Isn't it a Muslim name?" Maman added with hesitation.

Baba Nourie's face turned a little red and he turned away from Maman's face. His voice started to shake.

"Well…. Baba Nourie began sadly. "My father had a very rough time raising us in Esfahan. It was a constant battle between keeping our Jewish identity and dealing with some fanatic Muslims. The toughest day was when a group of local Muslim officials came to our door and forced my father to convert to Islam."

"Forced?" Maman interrupted.

"Yes, forced to say the Islamic decree by mouth and stop being a Joohood, since they believed all the Jews were born filthy," Baba Nourie said with intense frustration.

"My father," he continued, "had to say whatever he was asked to and declare that he had become a Muslim. But he never gave up his heart to it. He was so defenseless and cared about his family's safety. To further protect his children, he chose Muslim names for his sons.

"Now you know why my name is Noor-Allah, which means the Spirit of God," Baba Nourie declared in a louder voice.

"My other brothers' names are Faze-Allah and Rooh-Allah, and we all have the middle name Kalimi [Persian for Jewish]," he continued in a mocking tone. Baba Nourie proudly ended his story by saying, "Even though my father went through all these hassles, he was always devoted to his Jewish identity until his death."

Maman's eyes were filled with tears since her husband-to-be did not look happy anymore. Perhaps that was the first sign of her love for him. They both remained silent for several minutes until they heard Nana approaching them.

Nana announced with excitement that everything was in order and the wedding would take place soon.

The wedding ceremony was performed in Nana's house since there was always a fear of trouble from unwanted and hate-filled fanatical Muslim neighbors. The bride and groom looked lovely as could be under the Chuppah, the wedding canopy. The Rabbi came all the way from the northern part of Tehran to perform the Godly covenant. The Jewish blessings were expressed in beautiful Hebrew melodies and songs, and the glass cup was broken by the groom—symbolizing both the destruction of the temple in Jerusalem and their commitment to each other in future hard times. The repeating voices saying Mazel Tov and Mobarak-Basheh [Hebrew and Persian for happiness be with you] echoed throughout the wedding celebration. Everyone enjoyed dancing and eating very colorful and delicious food and sweets.

Now the teens were headed for a journey full of love, harshness, and some tragedies, but the wedding blessings would provide many miracles in their lives until death parted them.

CHAPTER THREE
BIRTH OF GITI

MAMAN WAS NEARLY FOURTEEN YEARS OLD when she felt a kick in her growing belly. She was puzzled. She remembered Nana being pregnant several times before, but she was never interested in asking any detailed questions about the pregnancy. It was awkward, Maman had thought back then, to ask how a baby had formed in her mother's belly and what to do when the baby is ready to come out. Now Maman, being pregnant herself, needed Nana's help to go over the pregnancy process.

"I don't quite remember how long a pregnancy lasts," Maman said to her mother.

"Nine months, more or less, but don't worry, Aziza-Joon

[dear Aziza], you'll know when you're ready to birth your baby," Nana answered sweetly. "There'll be periods of pain in the pregnancy months, but I am sure you can manage them. Just trust God to give you strength." Maman hugged her mother with a thankful heart.

"Just be with me, Nana, all the way through this pregnancy," Maman begged. Nana agreed and promised to be near her daughter most of the time.

Several months passed and finally Maman was ready to deliver her first child. The process of childbirth did not feel the same as Nana's instructions, so she panicked and begged her Nana and husband to stay near her. Nana calmly instructed Maman to push while lying down on a worn-out mattress on the floor. The young husband was excited even though he did not seem to know how to help his wife. He held her left hand and started caressing her sweaty dark hair with his other hand.

"Beh Omideh Khodah [With God's will] we will have a baby soon," Baba Nourie whispered aloud to his wife. After several hard pushes, a dark-skinned, dark-haired baby emerged from Maman. It was a girl. Upon her arrival, the baby powerfully kicked her arms and legs.

"Giti," Maman announced the name of her baby while panting with sweat running down her face. The name means "The World" in Persian, and since it was a whole world of joy for Maman to have this baby, it was the most appropriate name Maman could choose. There was no veto or arguments from Nana and Baba Nourie. Seeing the crying baby Giti in Maman's arms was the most beautiful moment for everyone. Soon Maman brought her precious baby to her breasts, which were filled with the tastiest food God had ever created other than manna [the Hebrew word for God's food provided to the Israelites in the wilderness for forty years]. Milk was flowing out of Maman's breast into baby Giti's tiny mouth, which helped to calm the baby's kicking and crying.

Baba Nourie was exhausted after several days of hard work selling eggplants on a wooden cart. Business was bad, but the good news of Giti's arrival wiped away all the tiredness and sadness of bringing home little money for the next meal, and replaced it with the joy and happiness of holding his first baby.

As Giti grew, she displayed a tomboy type of independence, and was sometimes hard to control. By age three, and still nursing, Giti sometimes acted as if she were in charge, but she also helped Maman with cleaning and preparing meals whenever food was available. Life was very hard since they had little food that lasted only a few meals a week, so Maman decided to continue to breastfeed Giti until she was close to four years of age to make sure her daughter was well fed. However, several months later, Maman had to refuse to continue breastfeeding since it started to hurt her breasts.

"But I want more," Giti begged Maman.

"No, Giti Joon, you are now a big girl and don't need your mother's milk," Maman replied gently.

Giti did not seem to be very happy about Maman's reply, so she kept repeating, "Why, Maman Joon, why?"

"I have another baby in my tummy, so I need to keep the milk for this baby," Maman answered. The exciting news of the new baby was enough for Giti to stop begging to be breastfed. She hugged and kissed Maman's belly for several minutes and left the room, jumping up and down!

Giti was a happy girl, still unaware of the harsh reality of life. Hunger, the deteriorating political situation, the stress of dealing with several Jew-hating neighbors, and many dangerous diseases were all around her.

Baba Nourie's eggplant-selling business was so slow

that there was no income, which meant no food or water (the water had been shut off due to unpaid bills). To make matters worse, Giti became very ill with a high fever. There were no doctors nearby, so Maman and Baba Nourie grabbed their sick child and took her to the nearest hospital on foot. When they reached the hospital, there were sick people lying all around in the corridors, with doctors and nurses scrambling to attend to the patients on a first-come, first-served basis. In one moment, Baba Nourie looked at Maman and their thoughts crossed into one idea: leave their little girl there and go home since they couldn't afford the expenses. Giti's crying would probably summon extra attention from the nurses. Her parents also feared the common practice of mistreatment of the Jews. The young parents told Giti that they would soon return and then left their child alone in the middle of the corridor. They left the hospital with heavy, breaking hearts. To their amazement, Giti did not mind being left there since she was a brave and independent girl.

The next day, Baba Nourie returned to the hospital and saw Giti playing with some dirt in the corner of the hospital corridor. She quickly ran to Baba and together they sneaked out of the hospital and quickly headed home. Maman was convinced that only her prayers to God had saved Giti's life.

Giti came home healthy after the one-day hospital adventure, as if nothing had happened. In fact, she was very thrilled to be home at Maman's side to help.

"What can I do to help you, Maman?" Giti asked while hugging her mother tightly.

"I am fine, my little darling helper," Maman replied.

"But Maman," Giti replied maturely, "I am not a little girl anymore; I am a big helper for you since Baba Nourie is not around often."

Giti received the same answer over and over from Maman— Ghorboonet Beram! [I die for you - an expression of deep love]

Giti was almost five years old when she approached Maman with a loving demand.

"Can I have a sister or brother soon, Maman Joon?" Giti asked. "Can God bring us a baby from Heaven and put it in your tummy, Maman? Can He?" she continued.

"I closed my eyes when you, Maman Joon, lit up the Sabbath candles last Friday night and asked God to give you a son," Giti said proudly. She paused for a moment and then continued by saying, "Or a sister, of course." But her heart was set on a brother.

Maman reached out to her daughter, lovingly grabbed her hands and started showering her with kisses.

"Ensha-Allah [God willing], Giti Joon, Ensha-Allah," Maman whispered into Giti's ears.

Several weeks later, Giti overheard her parents' conversation. Baba Nourie was holding his wife from behind while caressing her belly.

"How's my wife with a swollen belly filled with gas?" Baba Nourie jokingly whispered in Maman's ear. "Perhaps it was because you ate too much Ab-gousht at dinner!" Baba Nourie kept on teasing her. That was Baba Nourie's famous joke for pregnant women.

"It's not funny anymore." Maman turned around with a smile.

"We haven't had time to talk about it since Giti was very sick," Maman said. "But I am sure Giti will be delighted about this pregnancy," she continued with a proud smile.

Baba Nourie kept on rubbing Maman's belly gently. He then proudly admitted that he had been praying to God in his heart for a son after he finished reading the Siddur [Jewish daily prayer book] last Shabbat.

"I desperately want to see my son's Millah [circumcision]

and his Bar-Mitzvah before I die," Baba Nourie said excitedly.

As soon as Giti heard her father's wish, she could not contain herself and ran toward her parents with open arms to give them a hug. She then paused and looked at her parents with a puzzled expression.

"What is Milah or Barmis…what?… I don't get it?" Giti asked curiously.

Giti received her answer with loud laughter from her parents. "You'll find out, silly Giti," Baba Nourie replied. "Let's just pray and hope that the baby is a boy first."

Baba Nourie's heart was pounding out of happiness and his face was radiating with a wishful glow. His wish came true.

CHAPTER FOUR
BIRTH OF THE FIRST MORIS

Great Joys and Tragedies

Giti was counting the days impatiently. It became a daily habit to ask Maman the same questions: "Is the baby coming out today? How do you feel, Maman Joon? Can I talk to the baby now?"

Finally, the counting days and repeating questions were over and Giti was ready to meet her new sibling. She was a great help to her mother as Maman was giving birth. Giti would touch and kiss Maman's face and belly to comfort her, but the labor pain intensified by the minute.

"I want a brother," Giti kept repeating to Maman. Nana

came to her daughter's bedside and asked Giti to leave the room because the new baby was about to come out of the crying Maman. With a final push, Maman was able to deliver a fair-skinned, light-haired and light-brown-eyed baby boy. His features were the total opposite of Giti's features when she was born.

Baba Nourie could not believe his eyes the moment his utmost wish for a firstborn Jewish male came true. Totally speechless, he hugged his wife and the newborn at the same time while Nana called Giti to come in and see her new brother.

"A BOY!" Giti screamed with happy tears. "I knew it, I knew it."

Maman began nursing the baby and asked Giti to come alongside and say hello to her brother—Mousa [Hebrew name for Moris]. The chubby-cheeked baby boy was full of joy from the moment he arrived.

"God has answered my prayers for having a circumcision and a Bar-Mitzvah," Baba Nourie announced in a joyful tone.

"Yes He has, Khodarah-Shokr [thank God]," Maman replied. She then began to nurse baby Moris while Giti was near her.

Maman with baby Moris and Giti

"I am so glad, Maman Joon, that you have plenty of milk for my little brother now!" Giti said.

In spite of the great happiness they felt raising a son, things began turning from bad to worse. Baba Nourie worked very hard at many jobs to bring in money and feed his growing family. He had many good Muslim friends who didn't care about the political situation and had no negative opinions about any religious ideologies. They helped Baba Nourie with fruits and vegetables and they sometimes brought him a live chicken because they respected the tradition that the chicken should be butchered by a Rabbi for a Jewish family to eat.

Giti was practically a second mother for her brother Moris. She could not wait until the breastfeeding was over, so she could take care of her little brother while Maman was preparing meals. Bathing Moris was Giti's favorite chore. She helped Maman fill a small brass bowl with warm water and then she would grab a small washcloth to wash her little brother's body. Then that dreaded curious question came to Giti's mind as she was washing Moris' naked body—Millah [circumcision]!

"What is Millah?" Giti asked Maman. "You promised to tell me someday," she demanded.

"It is called circumcision, which is one of the most important Jewish things to do for a boy when he reaches eight days old," Maman informed Giti.

"But my little brother is older than that," Giti exclaimed. "Besides, I want to know everything about this circum… whatever," she stuttered.

Maman took a deep breath and gently lifted Moris' naked body out of the water and pointed to the baby's pubic area. "In a few days a Rabbi will come here to cut the extra skin of his pubic part as God commands us in Torah," Maman explained cautiously.

Maman was totally shocked that Giti was calm and did not interrupt with a girly scream. So she continued and asked Giti if she understood.

"Oh…yeah…" Giti replied quickly while washing Moris' body and staring at his private part. "I hope it won't hurt too much though," Giti said bravely.

Maman grabbed Moris and started drying him with a towel while Giti prepared the Ghondagh [a large cloth for wrapping the baby's legs together tightly—a Persian tradition and practice to keep the baby's legs from curving later on].

The circumcision was performed secretly and quickly by the local Rabbi, and once again, this Jewish ritual was satisfied according to God's command, and so was Giti's curiosity!

Several years of hunger and struggle passed, yet those years were filled with good memories. Maman continuously thanked and praised God for her family in spite of what little they had. The children, Giti and Moris, were best friends and brought great joy to the family. Their toys were dirt, stones, and twigs. Their one meal a day was a big event for them and in between, only imagination filled their minds and hungry tummies.

Moris was almost six years old when Baba Nourie brought home an amazing fruit—a watermelon! Baba Nourie grabbed a big knife, sliced into the melon and cut it into juicy portions for everyone.

Moris was staring at the reddish juicy watermelon portions filled with black seeds.

"I want the biggest one," Moris begged with his tender voice, while stretching his arms toward the pile of watermelon slices. Baba Nourie was busy cutting more chunks. Giti had already gone to a corner with several slices, and Maman was busy washing the dishes. Moris' begging stopped as soon as he was offered the biggest slice by his father.

Young Moris grabbed that huge chunk, ran away to a

corner and started biting into the melon's red flesh, not caring that he was eating the seeds. After several bites, he began to cough loudly. He wanted to run back to his family but he was helpless until it was too late. He fell face down to the ground. Maman was the first one to hear her son and ran to rescue him. The moment she saw young Moris choking, she frantically screamed for help. Moris' face quickly turned from red to blue. She was shocked and speechless standing near Moris as he was struggling to breathe. Baba Nourie grabbed his son's small body and ran outside, headed for the nearest hospital. He handed Moris' now limp body to the doctors and nurses and cried with his face to the ground. The doctors demanded that Baba Nourie stay out of the examining room.

After several hours of waiting, a doctor came out of the operating room toward Baba Nourie.

"I am so sorry that we could not rescue your son," the doctor announced quietly. "He is gone."

Baba Nourie started hitting his head and pulling his hair at the same time, which is a customary Iranian ritual showing the deepest pain of a loss.

"But it was only watermelon seeds!" Baba Nourie kept repeating with a loud cry. "Insha-Allah Bemiram [I hope to

God I die]." His loud voice filled the hospital corridor.

How could I go back home empty-handed? he thought to himself. But he had no choice. He had to take care of his soon-to-be saddened and broken-hearted family.

He came home with an exhausted soul and broken heart, unable to find any words of comfort for his devastated family. The moment Maman looked at her worn-out husband, her whole world came to an end. Her heart started pounding rapidly. Baba Nourie reached out to his crying wife and grabbed her tightly, but she managed to push him away and fell on the ground, sobbing intensely. She then began to strike her head and pull her hair as a way of showing traditional mourning for the loss of her loved one. It was tremendously painful for Baba Nourie to see his wife going through this agony. He grabbed Maman and tried to stop her from further harming herself, but she resisted. Baba Nourie didn't give up and continued his efforts to calm her down.

Giti was stunned at first, but that did not last long. She ran out of the room to a dark corner.

Maman finally gave up when there was no strength left in her. She leaned toward her husband's arms and collapsed. They both were too weak to even talk and search for Giti, but they knew she was somewhere in the house hiding and crying.

Toward the evening, Nana and several family members along with some Muslim neighbors came to visit the mourning family. Giti did not want to see anyone so she hid herself until dark. Nana finally found Giti and held her tightly without saying a word. Giti felt safe in Nana's arms and stopped crying. Several neighbors came to see Giti to comfort her with gentle hugs and kisses.

The agony of the loss of Moris brought together these loving neighbors and the family members, Jews and non-Jews. They all offered sincere heart-warming condolences and offered to provide food and support. Baba Nourie needed this support the most in order to stay close to his wife.

To make matters worse, Baba Nourie had to do the most difficult task that no father would ever wish to do—retrieve his son's body from the hospital and find a quick way of burying him. There was no designated Jewish cemetery in the area.

With a heavy heart and many tears, Baba Nourie headed back to the hospital and prayed that this nightmare would soon end. The people in charge of deceased patients pointed him to a cold room and gave him a white cloth. At that time each moment was passing in a frozen space in his mind, but with a praying heart and soul he managed to reach the room. He wrapped his beloved son's body in the white cloth, and left the hospital quickly.

He went to a remote area where there were no houses or buildings, nothing but weed-infested flat land with scattered tires and metal scraps. He dug out a small hole big enough for the body to fit into and enough space to cover it with dirt and weeds.

On the way back home, he was so overwhelmed with grief that he forgot the physical pain all over his body. Nothing was left except a painful soul.

Children are not supposed to die before their parents, Baba Nourie thought with a heavy heart. *Why this tragedy? Watermelon seeds? A gravesite with no tombstone, in the middle of nowhere?* Only God had a satisfying answer and whatever it was, He would deal with it. But Baba Nourie had to be strong for his wife, for Giti, and for the future he had promised his family. Whatever shred of hope that was left in his heart gave him a little strength to face his worn-out family.

After several hours, Baba Nourie came back home feeling drained, exhausted, and helpless to find any comforting words for his wife and daughter. Maman was sitting in a corner with Giti in her arms. They did not want to look at Baba Nourie and embrace the reality of the absence of Moris. Maman was praying to all the angels in Heaven to rescue her son, but they seemed to want Moris in Heaven after only such a short time on earth. Such a tragedy! Life now became meaningless to the family. Food had no taste, water did not satisfy thirst, there were no colors except black and gray, the sun looked dead, and dried-out eyes produced no more tears. Most tragically, their hearts lost all hope. There were no words to describe the pain of losing their firstborn son who had been so full of life.

During the next two years, life was a demanding force, moving on without any joy, yet Maman never lost her faith in God or His will and reason. There had to be a promise for the future.

Giti was devastated by the loss of her only playmate, but the support of Maman's love was so immense that Giti could go on playing and doing her school tasks. Baba Nourie promised his bride that God would provide comfort, and He did.

CHAPTER FIVE

BIRTH OF DAVOOD

SNOW WAS COMING DOWN HARD and covered the ground within minutes, while the blowing wind intensified. Safely tucked inside, the little family felt secure in their newly rented house, which felt like a mansion to them. Maman could now see a little color in life—hope.

"Come on in quickly, Giti Joon. I have great news for you," Maman yelled through the window overlooking the snow-covered ground.

Giti came into the house while blowing warm air onto her cold hands and rubbing her snow-covered shoes against a small Persian rug by the entry door.

"What is the good news, Maman?" Giti asked, shivering.

"A delicious Ghormeh-Sabzi dish and a loaf of your favorite bread, Noon-Sangag," Maman replied excitedly.

"This is one of my favorite foods, all the cooked greens, chunks of meat mixed with red kidney beans over Persian basmati rice," Giti said, salivating. "Where did you buy the Noon-Sangag? This brown bread is hard to find these days. I can't wait to eat it with the Ghormeh-Sabzi!"

"Baba Nourie worked for one of his friends and managed to barter for Noon-Sangag and some expensive meat for the Ghormeh-Sabzi," Maman replied.

Giti tucked herself under the Korsi and waited patiently for Maman to finish preparing the food.

Maman approached Giti and sat next to her under the Korsi.

"Here…come closer to me and touch my belly," Maman said with a smile.

"Are you sick, Maman?" Giti asked worriedly.

"No silly Giti," Maman replied with a slightly bigger smile. "Remember I told you about God and His angels?" Maman said gently.

But Giti immediately interrupted with a sad look on her face.

"I don't want to hear it anymore and don't say anything at all. I am still mad at God and His angels," Giti replied angrily while she tried to let go of Maman's belly.

"Wait...wait...Giti," Maman begged. "You have to stay and touch my belly more and then you'll get your answer."

In an instant Giti's angry face changed into a smiling one!

"You mean…you mean…there is a baby in there, Maman?" Giti said with great excitement.

Maman nodded with an even bigger smile.

Giti started kissing Maman's belly several times. She then got up quickly and started to jump up and down.

After going through the unimaginable tragedy of losing her son, seeing Giti's happiness gave Maman hope and a well-deserved smile. Maman's hope and smiles kept growing as the pregnancy continued. The anticipation for the birth of a new baby was the greatest remedy for Maman's broken heart, at least for part of it. Finally the day came!

When Maman was ready to birth her third child, she started repeating her quick prayer, "Beh Omideh To Khodah [to your will, God]."

With that in mind, she gained more power to push and gave birth to another baby boy with unexpected features:

blond hair and very light brown eyes.

So un-Jewish, Maman thought with a happy smile!

"Davood—I want this name for my boy," Baba Nourie announced with no objection from Giti. After all, this was a name from Torah—King David that is.

Everyone laughed in agreement.

"So what do you think of your new baby brother?" Maman asked Giti.

"I'm so happy to have Davood," Giti replied while touching his blond hair.

Giti promised herself she would watch out for this new baby Davood, and promised her parents, "No more watermelon, EVER!"

As Davood was growing up, Maman started to smile more often and enjoyed seeing both her husband and Giti being delighted by baby Davood. The new addition to Maman's life gave her strength to move on, even though the painful memories of Moris were still vivid in her mind.

The Jew-Town Move

Baba Nourie's business continued to struggle along with the political situation. Most Jews were afraid to be out in public, so they began moving to a place called Mahaleh [a Jewish town] located in a very poor and run-down area. Here some Jewish families shared a huge, very old building with multiple rooms throughout. This new housing, with a perfect square shape, looked like a 19th century castle. In the center was a huge yard surrounded by rooms, with several steps around each corner leading to the rooms. There were multiple faucets in the yard for public cleaning and washing since there were no showers. The most fascinating part of the décor was the huge old pomegranate tree in the center of the yard, making up an imaginary garden. Baba Nourie rented a huge room that had several tall windows containing small square panes of glass.

Nursing baby Davood gave Maman a taste of happiness and much hope for the future, even though not-too-distant memories of her firstborn son were constantly in her mind. She worked very hard preparing meals while Giti kept Davood busy nearby.

So many memories were made in Mahaleh that year with little food to eat and minimum entertainment for the children in the poor neighborhood. Even though the Shah of Iran had promised freedom for the Jews to attend synagogues and Jewish schools, there was always great fear when outside the perimeter of the Mahaleh.

Maman constantly warned her children to stay close to home. There was nothing as comforting and soothing as the arms of Maman whenever her children encountered mean, neighboring Muslim kids and adults who looked at the Jewish people with great hatred and resentment.

Maman was encouraged many times by her family members and Baba Nourie's brothers and sisters to move to Israel to live, but Maman loved her country of Iran, its culture, its language, and all her friends. "Zendegi Iran khoob hast [Persian for: Life in Iran is good]," Maman would often say over the years.

The Mahaleh way of life continued for a year and a half until Maman felt a kick in her tummy yet again.

CHAPTER SIX

A MIRACULOUS BIRTH—THE SECOND MORIS

BABA WAS SO EXCITED to see his young wife smiling while rubbing her swollen tummy again. After all, the only great news in Mahaleh came in the form of birth announcements.

Giti and Davood were jumping up and down from the excitement of having another sibling. Even though Davood was nearly three years old, he was aware of the fact that there was a baby growing in his mother's belly—thanks to Giti informing her brother of so many facts of life.

When the due date arrived, a midwife came to assist Maman's birth process.

"No children around me please," the midwife announced. Giti obeyed and grabbed her little brother and took him out of the room so he could not hear Maman's crying.

"It's a boy!" the midwife announced.

"But wait," Maman said excitedly, "it's not just a boy, but an unbelievable miracle!" Had God answered Maman's tearful prayers to bring back her first Moris? But how was it possible? Was Maman dreaming? Even the new baby's crying sounded the same. After cleaning the baby, he now looked one hundred percent like their firstborn son Moris! Both Baba Nourie and Maman cried and hoped that no one would wake them up from their dream.

Baba Nourie called Giti and Davood to come in quickly. As soon as Giti saw the new baby she was stunned!

"Yah-Khodah… Yah-Khodah [Oh my God]," Giti kept repeating in amazement. "Now I am not mad at God and His angels anymore since my first little brother came back from Heaven," Giti said proudly. Everyone laughed.

This is the confirmation of the miracle, Maman thought.

Giti held the miracle baby in her arm gently and looked at Maman with tearful eyes.

"What now?" Maman asked Giti while continuing to laugh. "You got your brother now and I'm sure you'll take care of him soon," she said.

Giti looked up and stared at Maman's face, and before Giti could begin to talk, Maman read Giti's mind and said: "Absolutely yes, we'll name the baby Moris." It was as if the angels in Heaven had mercy on Maman for her trust in God and they brought Moris back to her. But how was this possible? Maman did not question or want to know.

Davood didn't care about all the talking going on. He just stood near Maman and stared at his new baby brother.

"Did you hear that, Davood?" Giti asked while holding the new Moris in her arms like a doll. "I have my little brother back again and together we'll keep him safe," Giti continued.

Davood shrugged his shoulders and said, "Ok!" Maman held the baby tightly in her arms for several minutes, just to be certain of the reality of his birth. She then began nursing Moris with great joy.

The family circle was growing, and as it did Giti acted more and more like a tomboy. Davood was happy to roll a torn tire down the dirt road, hitting it with a large stick, and the second baby Moris was nursing constantly. Maman always stared at the baby while nursing, praising God and thanking His angels for bringing her firstborn son back. *Khoda-Ra Shokr* [Thank God].

Giti and Davood felt some jealousy as they watched Maman with baby Moris "glued" to her body most of the time, but didn't let it bother them since they noticed that Maman was smiling a lot more than before.

Sicknesses, Political Mayhem, and More Miracles

The second Moris was almost three when he developed an unusual fever one night. His screams were agonizing and out of control. Maman tried not to lose her composure and allow the painful memories to destroy her life. Intense nursing didn't help and the baby was growing weaker. Baba Nourie told his crying wife that there was an old Muslim man living outside Mahaleh who could help.

"I never met this man before, but we have no other choice," Baba Nourie said frantically. He carried young Moris (who had no strength to scream anymore) and Maman followed. All of them were barefoot in their rush to get help.

The alleys were very dark, but that did not cause Maman and Baba Nourie to slow down.

"Where is the old man's house?" Maman cried.

"Just a couple more alleys ahead of us," Baba Nourie

assured his wife. "Just keep your voice down and trust God to show us the way." But Maman did not listen and kept on crying and showed no fear of confronting anybody. The crying woke some Muslim neighbors and brought them out of their houses to investigate. The number of awakened men and women kept growing as an increasing number of grumbling voices could be heard.

"Hey, what's going on here?" a Muslim woman shouted while approaching the crying Maman. But Maman kept on crying and Baba Nourie did not want to even look at the woman's face to avoid any offensive misunderstanding.

"Wait here now," the woman told Maman and headed back to her house quickly to bring her husband, who seemed to be annoyed by the noise.

Well, God, if you want us dead now, let it be, Maman thought.

"Our son is very sick and we are looking for a doctor who lives nearby," Baba Nourie begged the man. "Do you know where we can find him?"

"You know these are Joohoods [filthy Jews] from Mahaleh?" the angry man alerted his wife, ignoring Baba Nourie's begging.

"Yes, I know they are," the motherly Muslim woman

yelled at her husband.

"Come on, I think I know where the doctor's house is," the Muslim woman told Maman, ignoring her husband's obvious hatred. "Just follow me and I'll take you to the doctor's house. It's not too far," she assured them.

The small crowd disappeared quickly and the angry husband went inside and slammed the door.

"Tashakor… Tashakor [Persian polite way of saying thank you]," Maman told the Muslim woman while giving her a hug. The woman disappeared into the darkness.

When Baba Nourie found the house, he gently knocked on the door several times. After a few minutes, an old man in his pajamas opened the door. Without asking any questions, he immediately invited Maman and Baba Nourie to come in. This compassionate Muslim man brought a candle and then opened a box full of used needles and syringes. With his bare hands, he picked up one of the needles and attached it to the syringe. He held the needle over the candle's flame to sterilize it and then filled the syringe with a liquid and injected it into the baby's bottom. The pain of the injection gave the baby the strength to scream. Maman fainted and was unconscious for several minutes. When she regained consciousness, she immediately began praying to God while squeezing her weak baby in her arms.

"I will not allow this baby to go back to Heaven," she pleaded to God. After Moris had rested for several hours, the old man was amazed to see a large worm come out of the baby's rectum. As disgusting as it looked, this was great news.

"Whatever that liquid in the syringe was, it worked magically or miraculously," Maman proclaimed.

They thanked the old Muslim man and praised God for allowing this man to be available nearby. For that moment in time, there was no Jew, no Muslim, no one. They felt a trust in humanity and in the presence of God.

Moris slept for hours after the horrific experience and Maman cried out to God with thanks, her arms in the air.

This baby Moris was growing up to look just like the first Moris. Despite the poverty around them, the family members' hearts were full of richness and happy moments.

But despite the happy days and the extra attention to baby Moris, the family experienced yet another painful ordeal.

One evening Maman was finishing up cleaning the room and making sure everyone was inside for the night. Giti and Davood were busy playing with some colorful papers they had found outside. Baba Nourie was out of the house and was expected to be home late. The air in the room was dry and stuffy, so Maman lit a kerosene heater and placed a small metallic bowl filled with water on top of the heater to boil in order to moisturize the air. After several minutes, vapor started to appear from the bowl. Baby Moris was fascinated and watched the water vapor oozing out from the top of the heater. Maman noticed some glass dishes in the kitchen so she hurried back to put them away, but it was too late. She heard an excruciating scream. She quickly turned around and saw the boiling water all over Moris' arms. Everyone was startled by the scream and ran toward Maman and Moris to figure out what happened.

Maman tried very hard to soothe Moris' burnt hands by running cold water over them, but his screaming intensified.

"How can it be?" cried Maman to God. "First the watermelon, then the high fever, and now the burning water. I don't know if I can bear any more of these awful things happening to my baby."

The blisters on Moris' hands began to look better as Maman tried to remedy them with cold water and some mystery ointment handed down by Nana. The baby's crying subsided as he rested in Maman's arms and listened to the sweet sound of her voice praying to God.

Maman devoted her attention to this young Moris around the clock. She even kept him near her all through the night. Giti and Davood kept each other busy, playing in the dirt and throwing stones. Soon, school began in the very small Jewish school outside Mahaleh. The Jewish community was quite safe most of the time, but once any family member left their safe place, they encountered looks of hatred and disgust.

Despite the painful animosities, there were several compassionate Muslim families living nearby who were peaceful and loving people. Most of them were nurses and healthcare workers. They worked in an old hospital alongside Jewish doctors and nurses. Once someone stepped into the hospital, there were no Jews or Muslims or Armenians or even Atheists. There were only human beings seeking help.

The political situation, however, was getting worse—not just for the Jews, but for everyone. Maman warned her children not to stay out too late, and most importantly, to come home as soon as school ended each day. There were no buses or any other transportation for the children, so they went to school and back home on foot.

Moris was in the second grade when there was a surprise announcement from the school office. A movie was being offered for all students to watch after school that day. It was such great news to young Moris, since the children had never attended a movie before. He happily agreed to stay after school, forgetting Maman's warning. Time was frozen inside Moris' head as soon as the last school bell rang. The excitement of watching a movie was the only thing on his mind. The movie seemed to be a short one, but upon stepping out of the school building, Moris could see that the sky had grown dim. His heart seemed to stop when he saw the long, dark shadows in front of him. Tears started to pour from his eyes as his hands began to tremble.

How could I ignore my Maman's warning? How can I walk home? Is it too late to rush home? Moris thought with terror.

All of the parents and children slowly disappeared from the school, ignoring the lonely Moris staring at the exit door. They had to leave quickly since it was getting dark rapidly and all the Jews were careful not to be out late. The principal was nowhere to be seen, which added to Moris' fear.

Maman will kill me for sure, Moris kept thinking, which made him cry for help. So he hid in the corner of the schoolyard, hoping to wake up from this nightmare. After several minutes, his head racked with guilt, he saw a black chador [Persian for a Muslim tent-like covering for women] -covered woman rushing toward him. As she got closer, Moris could hear a whimpering cry that sounded just like Maman's. It WAS Maman! There was a tall, muscular man behind her who looked like a bodyguard. Maman screamed at Moris and scolded him for not obeying her orders.

"I couldn't find your father so I had to ask one of his friends to accompany me for a safe walk to school," Maman screamed while scolding her crying son. But soon she stopped her screaming, grabbed Moris and hugged him under her chador. Moris was comforted by his mother's hugs and kisses and especially her repeated words, "Ghorboonet Beram [I die for you]." Maman finally let go of him and warned him to obey her rules.

"How many more of these awful events can I tolerate for this child?!" Maman started to cry to both her son and God.

"We must hurry," Baba Nourie's friend Hassan interrupted Maman as they exited the schoolyard. He told her that there were several violent demonstrations going on all over the city and warned Maman to hurry home. He had to return to his home immediately and left Maman with Moris, so they had to run home by themselves. Within minutes, they could hear "Marg-bar-Joohood" [Persian for "Death to the filthy Jews"] chants ahead of them. Before they thought about changing direction, the violent crowd got very close to them. Everybody was running in all directions, trying to stay away from the mad mob. Most of the men were riding bikes and trying to run down other people, especially the women. In one awful moment, a bike rider raced alongside Maman and grabbed her chador, removing it from her head violently. Maman's long reddish-black hair then fell down around her neck and was visible under the streetlights. The bikers got even angrier when they saw this Jewish woman with exposed hair, so they began to spit on her and chant anti-Jewish slogans. Maman wiped the spit off her face with one hand and with the other she held on tightly to her terrified young son. She raced back and forth, forcing her way out of the chaos to find her chador before she could be executed in front of her son.

She saw her chador on the ground in the middle of the chaotic crowd. It was being trampled on and dragged. She held on tightly to Moris' hand and walked toward her chador. At the same time, the angry biker moved toward her for his assault, but within seconds he was pushed aside by the force of the incoming bikers. Maman cried out loudly and thanked God for His miraculous act that had saved them from a tragic attack. She managed to retrieve her chador to cover herself and looked for a safe spot. They crossed the street into a dark alley and stayed there for a while to make sure there was no sign of angry bikers.

The streets seemed fairly quiet and safe to walk, even though they could hear from some distance distraught people looking for their loved ones. Maman gained enough strength to walk fast toward home while holding her terrified son.

When Maman and Moris finally returned home, they were both so shaken and exhausted that they went straight to bed without saying anything to the rest of the family members. That night was a very restful one for Moris as he was tucked in close to Maman's side all night long.

"Khodah Ra Shokr [Persian for thank God]," Maman whispered all through the night.

CHAPTER SEVEN
BIRTH OF KAMRAN

AS MAMAN WAS PLUCKING a butchered chicken for the preparation of several meals, she thought about her first son, Moris. He was always fascinated watching feathers coming off a dead chicken. He often used to catch some of the small flying feathers in the air.

Perhaps I should quit making chicken meals to avoid this memory, Maman thought tearfully, but she changed her mind since her Jewish chicken soup—well-known as Jewish Aspirin—was one of the favorite meals for her family when they were sick with cold or flu. She looked at her belly with a smile. Another baby was on the way.

Before the mixture of happy and sad tears flew down

Maman's cheeks, Baba Nourie came home with a loud "Salam Azizam [Persian for hello my dear]."

"Why are you home early?" Maman asked with a worried smile.

"I brought some delicious red apples for which I bartered with my friends so you can make Faloodeh Seeb [shredded apple slices in icy water mixed with honey]," Baba Nourie replied.

"But Yom Kippur is a month away, you silly husband!" Maman said. Iranian Jews are known to break their fast at the end of Yom Kippur with Faloodeh Seeb.

"Did you find a new job? Or perhaps you brought some lamb meat we have needed for months?" Maman kept asking.

"No Azizam, I want to celebrate another promise of God to us—our new birth announcement," Baba Nourie replied with a big smile.

By now the news of another pregnancy was not as surprising as it used to be, but it was a great distraction from the bitter reality of life.

Maman tried not to disappoint her happy husband, so she washed her hands and started to make the Faloodeh Seeb while she was selfishly thinking about the wished-for lamb meat. She couldn't remember the last time she tasted some. Perhaps that was during her wedding? She started shredding the apple into a glass bowl of ice water mixed with honey. She noticed at the same time that Baba Nourie was gently touching her belly.

"I am asking God to give us another girl this time," Maman told her husband while enjoying the warmth of his hands on her belly.

"Giti has been begging me for a sister," Maman added. "By now she is probably tired of taking care of two boys and wants to be more girly than a tomboy. Who knows?"

Baba Nourie didn't pay much attention to what Maman was saying since he was staring at the big bowl of Faloodeh Seeb with anticipation and enjoying touching his wife's warm belly.

As soon as the Faloodeh Seeb was ready, Baba Nourie stopped caressing Maman's belly, grabbed a big spoon and scooped a large chunk of the icy honey-sweetened apple shreds. "Tastes great! Feels like Yom Kippur again," Baba Nourie said, with some of the apple shreds stuck to his mustache.

The husband and newly pregnant wife enjoyed their relaxing time alone together while tasting the Faloodeh Seeb.

They were both quiet but were thinking about the new baby soon to be added to the family. The quiet time did not last long! The kids barged into the room like a hungry troop demanding food and drink.

Everyone enjoyed the Faloodeh Seeb treat and lay down on the floor to take a nap while waiting for their next meal.

"Wait a minute," Giti said curiously while lying down on the floor. "This is not Yom Kippur, what's going on with this Faloodeh Seeb treat now?" Her parents could not answer Giti right away since they were enjoying the treat. After they finished eating, they smiled at all the children and announced the good news of another pregnancy.

The children looked at each other while having their cups of Falloodeh Seeb, and within seconds they all dropped their treats on the floor and started jumping up and down. The boys then started to roll over back and forth. After several minutes of happy movements, they cleaned their mess and once again they began the family ritual of rubbing Maman's belly and giving it kisses.

The happy day ended with drinking Falloodeh Seeb to the last drop and waiting anxiously for Maman's chicken meal, which took more than two hours.

Life within Mahaleh remained the same. The pomegranate tree gave more reddish fruit and the children enjoyed climbing the tree and picking the fruit and fighting over each piece. As the nights turned colder, Maman and Baba Nourie made sure that each child had a fair share of blankets, since the family was lying down together in a row on the floor. When the Korsi was available, everyone huddled around it with their bodies tucked under the heavy blankets that covered the Korsi. It truly was a miracle that no one suffocated from the trapped carbon monoxide generated by the hot coals in the center of the Korsi.

Maman could feel that this baby was different from the others. Throughout the pregnancy the baby was kicking so hard that Maman predicted that she might go into labor long before the due date. She almost felt like she was carrying twins since she felt pain throughout her insides. Everyone in the family was amused by the moving bumps all over Maman's belly.

"These are the baby's kicks, children," Maman told them while smiling and trying not to show the pain. Davood and Moris were afraid to touch Maman's belly now, but Giti was entertained not only by touching Maman's belly, but also by putting her ears on the belly to listen.

The baby's kicks were unbearable by the eighth month, and Maman announced, "This baby must be a boy and he will make a great soccer player in his lifetime!"

"But I want a baby sister," Giti replied with some disappointment while resting her head on Maman's belly.

"What makes you think this is definitely a boy?" Maman replied while touching Giti's hair.

"Well…you said a soccer player," Giti replied. "So it must be a boy and cannot be a girl then," Giti added with a defiant attitude.

"You know you are right, Giti Joon," Maman said with a puzzled voice. "I can't believe a girl could play soccer. After all, it is impossible to conceive of a grown woman playing soccer." She imagined a bunch of women with chadors playing soccer in a field. That made Maman giggle!

She gently grabbed Giti's face and looked straight into her eyes. "Boy or girl, you will make a great mother's helper again, as always," Maman said very proudly.

Giti smiled with great joy and covered Maman's belly with the blanket.

"Well I don't want my baby soccer player to catch a cold

now," she said.

A few weeks later, the labor pains came all of a sudden, but Maman didn't mind since she wanted to be free of the kicks.

"Quick…get the midwife now!" Maman woke up her husband in the middle of the night, panting. "And please don't wake anybody up!"

But it was too late, since the family's long, heavy blanket on the floor was too crowded with the kids close to the parents. Baba Nourie got up quickly, trying to walk past the row of sleepy kids. He unintentionally stepped on Giti's toes, which woke her up.

"Shhh…Maman is in labor now, so please stay near your mother quietly until I come back with the midwife. The boys should not wake up and make noises as Maman requested." Giti happily agreed.

"Ok…Maman Joon," Giti said quietly. "I'll bring some washcloths with warm water to rub your head to make you feel better." Maman gave Giti a smile as the panting and pains became more rapid.

Maman thought for a moment in between the labor pains: *Why do I even bother with the midwife since I have my expert right here next to me?*

Giti started to gently rub Maman's forehead with a warm wet washcloth. She whispered to Maman to hang in there until the midwife arrived.

After nearly an hour, the midwife showed up and was amazed at how Giti was taking care of her mother during labor. The midwife presented her demand again to Baba Nourie—no children around Maman. The midwife asked that he move them to the other side of the room or under the Korsi. Giti and her father obeyed and moved the kids away from the birthing area.

"A dark-skinned baby boy!" announced the midwife. Maman wasn't all that surprised since she remembered the strong kicks during her pregnancy.

"Just look at his movements," the midwife noticed. The movements of his hands and legs were fascinating, as if he were looking for a soccer field to make the final goal. Everyone was delighted to see a new baby, and at the same time they were amazed by the movements of his hands and legs.

"Ok, Giti Joon," Maman said happily, "go for it and name your brother now!"

Giti was so excited by this and immediately said: "Kamran!"

"Where did you get this name?" Maman asked.

"I know this kid named Kamran in the neighborhood who is obsessed with soccer. Besides, I know my new little brother is going to be a soccer star," Giti replied.

"Then Kamran it is!" both parents agreed.

All of the siblings screamed with happiness and stared at Kamran's naked body and laughed. Maman gladly offered a full milky breast to the new baby and began saying "*Ghorboonet Beram* [Persian for I would die for you]" as an expression of deep love as she had been doing for all of her kids at their births.

The family welcomed the new soccer player with plenty of hugs and kisses until the morning hours. They all went to bed with a unanimous thought: *Thank God for another joy in our lives*.

Baby Kamran grew up very quickly and began walking before he turned one year old. He discovered his favorite food: Dirt! No one could prevent him from eating it. He played with nothing but dirt and gravel. The one thing he hated was shoes, so being barefoot made him happy. By the age of three, Maman's prediction proved to be right. Baby Kamran wanted to kick everything that had a round shape. A torn plastic ball was his winning trophy and nothing made him happier. Maman was proud of young Kamran's independence, but sometimes it was too much for her to see her son get hurt playing with large stones and get cut by sharp objects he discovered in the dirt piles.

One day Maman heard a loud scream in the yard. She was very familiar with that scream. It was Kamran on the ground, crying very hard while holding his head. She discovered that he had been challenged by the other kids to pick up a heavy rock that had sharp edges and throw it up in the air without moving. It was a crazy and meaningless challenge, and the only volunteer was young Kamran. Apparently, the stone landed on his head and left a large, bloody goose-egg bump. Maman washed the bump and applied an icy-cold washcloth to it for several minutes. After an hour of resting, Kamran wanted to return outside, but this time without participating in any challenging games.

While Maman watched her children play outside, she wondered what the future would hold for the remaining Iranian Jews. Many with money had fled the country and now resided in Israel or America. But Maman's heart continued to feel she belonged in Iran with the language, the culture, and her neighbors—both Jews and some nice Muslims.

"Burn the Jews" and Homelessness

One day, Maman heard an angry mob from a distance as they were approaching Mahaleh. She could clearly hear the clamoring chants of "Marg bar Joohood [Death to the filthy Jews]." She hurriedly searched for all her children and found everyone nearby except Moris. She ran outside Mahaleh and called loudly for her son.

"Where are you?" Maman frantically screamed. Everyone was running around to avoid the coming mob. Some teens did the opposite. They wanted to have a closer look and watch the excitement. Maman kept on moving, calling for her son. She could clearly hear many parents screaming for their loved ones as well. Cries of "Ya-Khoda, Ya-Toorah [Oh God, Oh Torah]" were echoing everywhere, which added extra fuel to the anti-Jewish mob.

The mob was now in a narrow alley near the hospital, and people were screaming and running away from them. Some people fell and were trampled by the running crowd. As the mob neared the hospital, its ringleader had a huge stick in his hand and hatred flamed from his eyes. He climbed over the huge stone sign in front of the hospital door and ordered his followers to break all the windows and then burn all the Jews inside the building. Maman saw beaten, bloody people scrambling into the alley, running for their lives. Next, she heard loud breaking glass all around the hospital, adding to her fear of losing Moris. There was no sign of her missing son anywhere. Maman's heart started beating faster than she could bear. She needed God's presence immediately to end this chaos. So she prayed while looking frantically for her lost boy. After more than an hour, her prayers were answered. Her son was hidden behind a tall dirt wall at the end of the alley. She called his name immediately, but he could not move. Maman grabbed her son and held him tightly in her arms.

"What on earth are you doing out here?" Maman asked with eyes full of tears. Moris was still speechless and shocked. Maman didn't expect an answer and realized that there was no time to stay in that alley. The mob was still chanting very loudly while continuing to damage the hospital. Maman had to make a quick decision about how to escape from that mayhem. She hid Moris under her chador and carefully zigzagged through the running crowd. Her mind was racing with awful things that could happen, but she trusted God to lead her out of this chaos and provide a safe way home. She needed a miracle—a miracle like she remembered from Torah when the Israelites reached the Red Sea and realized that there was no way to escape from the vicious enemy behind them. The powerful hands of God parted the Red Sea and made a safe passage for all the Jews. Maman needed a safe passage home too.

Once she managed to get out of the crowd, she heard the ringleader's loud announcement. "Don't go inside the hospital since there are some Muslim doctors and nurses working there. We have caused enough damage," he ordered. The mob stopped their destruction and quickly scattered in different directions. As the ringleader was walking away from the stone sign in front of the hospital, Maman turned around and saw his hate-filled face and the damage he and his followers left behind. He then left the scene and quickly disappeared.

That was the miracle Maman needed at that moment. She thanked God and headed home with a thankful heart.

Perhaps fleeing Iran is not such a bad idea, Maman thought for a moment, but her heart did not listen. Maman grabbed her stunned son and carried him home without saying a word.

Baba Nourie came home to a tearful wife and that broke his heart. It was time for the family to move to some other place, but there was nowhere to go since the business was nearly bankrupt.

Baba Nourie gave the bad news the next day.

"There is no money, period!"

Maman was still in bed resting with Moris, trying to forget the awful memories from the previous day. She needed strength to move on with life after what had happened. The images of yesterday's events raced through her mind, especially the face of the ringleader.

How could any human being be filled with such destructive hate? she thought. *What would his family think of him, if he has any?*

Baba Nourie noticed how Maman was stressed out, but he had to tell his wife the news.

"Did you hear what I just said?" he asked Maman quietly. "We have to do something about it soon."

"But where do we go from here?" Maman replied. Baba Nourie asked his wife to get up and go to the kitchen for further talk.

"I know a trustworthy Muslim friend who can help us

for a while," Baba Nourie told her. "He said we can move to an empty storage room in the factory where he works until we can afford to find a place to live," he continued. "But we can only stay during the nights after he is done working every day, so we would be out during the day."

"You mean being homeless?" Maman asked. Baba Nourie nodded and promised to find someplace else soon, but fulfillment of his promise took a little longer than expected.

For nearly two and a half years, the family lived in a large factory room by night and wandered throughout the city by day. Sometimes they stayed with Nana and some distant family members for several hours a day, but it was too bothersome for their relatives to take care of the whole family. They had to go back to the room in the factory at nighttime.

Despite the painful days they endured, Maman tried to make sure her children had fun and made good memories. The funniest memory Maman would later recall was the low ceiling height of the factory room where only the children could stand up. Maman and Baba Nourie had to stoop down in order to walk around. Many times, they forgot and hit their heads on the low ceiling, which made everyone laugh.

"The God of Torah is full of mercy!" Maman cried out

when she heard that her husband could work for his brother Fayzolah, who had recently opened a small dry cleaning business. Life began transitioning from a deep darkness to a bright light, from hopelessness to some hopefulness, from tears to happy faces, from dingy gray to bright colors!

"How many miracles do we deserve from God and how many praises should we announce to our God?" Maman wondered aloud. The growing family moved to a large room in an old house where another extra miracle happened—Maman was pregnant again.

CHAPTER EIGHT

BIRTH OF LILI— A NANOO-BABY!

MAMAN REQUESTED THAT HER HUSBAND make a huge Nanoo [Persian for hammock] inside the room in which they were living. He agreed and bought a heavy-duty blanket and attached ropes to two opposite corners and nailed them to the walls.

The children were amazed while they were watching their father building the mysterious thing being hung on the walls.

"What is that?" Davood asked. "A giant swing thingy?"

"It is a surprise for your mother, a Nanoo," Baba Nourie said, and warned the children how it should be handled.

Maman was delighted to see this Nanoo and made the announcement of her pregnancy. Everyone shouted for joy and reached out to Maman's belly and started talking to their new sibling. They all wanted a girl since it seemed like there were too many boys around.

"As you can see," Baba Nourie continued, "this is for the new baby only."

"Can we swing the Nanoo when the baby is in it?" the boys asked at the same time.

"Yes you can swing the Nanoo sometimes, but only under the supervision of your mother or Giti," he replied in a stern voice.

Giti smiled at Baba Nourie's demand, but was doubtful that the boys would obey the rule fully. She brought three long pillows and placed them underneath the Nanoo just in case the boys swung it hard and the baby fell off the Nanoo.

Maman and Baba Nourie were both delighted to see Giti's action for the safety of the baby.

"She is my second mother indeed!" Maman announced happily.

While Baba Nourie was inspecting the hooks on the walls to ensure the safety of the Nanoo, Maman and the children were busy decorating inside the Nanoo with small pillows and a baby blanket.

Everyone took a last look at the hung Nanoo and went to bed happy.

"I certainly pray for a girl," Maman whispered to her husband in bed. "I miss combing the hair of a baby girl, just like when Giti was a little girl."

"I sure hope for a girl too," Baba Nourie replied. "I really do."

The pregnancy was a quiet one with no soccer-playing kicks, no twisting, and no pain at all.

When the pregnancy days were over, Maman was quite comfortable with the birthing process. The baby girl came quickly with no crying.

Did this baby sleep all through these nine months of pregnancy? Maman wondered. Maman stared at the quiet baby in her arms. The baby had light skin, big brown eyes, fluffy black hair, and an adorable pug nose on her chubby face.

"She looks like my chubby Aroosak [Persian for a doll] I used to have when I was a little girl," Maman announced. Everyone smiled.

"Who wants to name this chubby Aroosak now?" Maman asked.

At first, no one said anything. Then Giti jumped up and

announced: "Lili!"

"A perfect name for an Aroosak!" Baba Nourie replied. But Maman showed some tender mercy and asked the boys, who were giggling at their new sister, if they liked the name Giti had picked.

"Ahhh…sure why not," the boys replied, shrugging their shoulders. And the man in charge, Baba Nourie, showed his approval by a group hug with Giti, the baby, and his worn-out wife.

The motherhood experience started again. Constant nursing and taking care of the baby's needs seemed joyful chores for Maman. The siblings took turns, amid lots of fights, swinging the Nanoo with baby Lili in it.

As Giti predicted, a couple of times the boys swung the Nanoo too high, which caused the baby to fall off and land on the soft pillows underneath, thanks to Giti for placing the pillows before. To everyone's surprise, Lili didn't cry, acting as if nothing happened! But Maman and Giti warned the boys to avoid strong swings.

Besides being an excellent cook, Maman had a gift for knitting too. She could knit without even looking at her fingers as they moved the needles around and pushed the multicolor yarn in many directions. A beautiful sweater could be formed in a matter of hours. She could knit while waiting for a meal to cook, watching her children play, and ordering them not to fight.

Although Maman never minded Giti's behavior as a tomboy, she wanted to see Lili grow up to be more girlish. Giti helped Maman constantly with baby chores, especially dressing Lili with tender loving care. Giti wanted to be both a mother and father to the baby, since Baba Nourie was out most of the time making ends meet.

The one-room "home" seemed smaller every day since everybody wanted to be with the baby most of the time. They occupied the room all the time, making messes and demanding food around the clock. Life was getting on Maman's nerves sometimes since she had little room to do her work.

Lili was almost nine months old when Maman thought it was time to disassemble the Nanoo. Everyone agreed.

Maman was thankful to have more room to move around comfortably, but mostly grateful to God for having a place to live and children who were content with what little they had.

Several years passed and God's mercy started pouring into the family circle. There was plenty of good news—Baba

Nourie's business was growing, which generated more money, and the political situation was better for the Iranian Jews. It was time to fulfill a dream: Moving to another dwelling that was an actual house.

"You'll be amazed at how spacious the house is," Baba Nourie told his wife proudly. The children heard their father's announcement and thought about the biggest house they could imagine.

Finally a house that had a real address! When Baba Nourie announced the news of moving to a new house, his description of the dwelling turned out to be an understatement. Everyone's eyes were wide and they had no words to express the true happiness in their hearts when they arrived at what they called "The Mansion." Everyone thought this was the description Baba Nourie should have used in his announcement!

CHAPTER NINE

THE ARIANAH MANSION

"THE MANSION" HAD TWO STORIES with two small rooms on each level. One of the upstairs rooms was attached to something else Iranians dream of—a balcony! The final magical touch was a yard with two rectangular gardens filled with beautiful green weeds. The children could not contain their excitement! They screamed, danced, and jumped up and down during the entire moving day. Lili, almost four years old, found herself in a magical kingdom where everyone was happy and no longer hungry.

This magical "mansion" was in the northern part of Tehran called Arianah. There was a huge, flat, barren stretch of land behind the house, ready to be used for building more "mansions." However, there was no sewer system yet in place, so unsanitary fluids were flushed through the narrow ditches around the houses and flowed downstream to a very deep hole several miles away. The Muslim neighbors didn't bother the Jewish families since all the neighborhood children played and swam *together* in the dirty sewage-filled mini-streams.

Maman constantly looked at the first dream she had begged God to give her for years—the kitchen! She tried to decorate with the few belongings she had. She also wanted to fix the weed-filled garden and grow her favorite rose flowers and some vegetables, but there was so little time since she had to constantly wash the children's filthy clothes and cook to satisfy the happy family.

Choking Bird, Shaking Ground and Hallucinations

She had a very tiny body with fair skin and puffy cheeks like a doll, just as Maman had described Lili when she was born. She always had a smile on her face. Even the bacteria-filled sewer fluid all over her hands and face did not stop that doll-face from smiling. She always seemed to get along with the other kids, and they all loved to swim in the mini-streams together.

The other siblings spent hours in the barren area playing soccer games, digging through dirt, and smashing bugs. The kids never felt strange or unsafe with the Muslim kids since there were plenty of distractions in the field.

Plenty of memories were made at the Arianah home. Maman was the "*Shah-Banoo* of the mansion [Persian for queen]" since her husband was treating her like one by bringing her plenty of colorful vegetables and fruits and meat. He started to call Maman Shahbanooyeh Man [my queen] while proudly hugging and kissing her. For the first time since they were married, Maman could now prepare three meals each day.

One day, Baba Nourie brought home a fat live turkey, which was a big surprise for everyone.

"This turkey is not to be used as a pet in the house," Maman announced. "We're going to find a Rabbi to butcher it for plenty of hot meals!"

Maman's announcement was upsetting to the kids, who really wished to keep the bird as their house pet.

"Can we at least keep it for a while? We promise to take care of it. Please?" the kids begged.

Maman asked Baba Nourie for advice about the kids' request. Baba Nourie was busy cleaning the bird's feathers and other mess that was left on his clothes during delivery.

"Why not? Let the kids have fun keeping the bird. Besides, it'll take a while to find a Rabbi," Baba Nourie told Maman.

Maman agreed and told the kids the good news. Everyone cheered and promised to clean up after the bird.

It was quite a challenge to have a turkey as a pet in the house, but the kids deserved a chance to make funny memories for several days. Maman recalled one of her favorite and funniest memories.

One day Lili screamed from downstairs and Maman rushed down the steps to find the turkey choking on something. Lili told Maman that the birdie ate a big thing from off the floor. When Maman looked around, she found a broken bag of whole walnuts scattered on the counter. Maman grabbed the bird and felt its neck where a large round object was stuck. She then gently massaged the walnut downward toward the bird's stomach. The nearly-dead bird started to flap its huge wings and made funny noises, as if crying for help. After several attempts, Maman finally managed to push the walnut all the way down to its stomach so that the bird could breathe again. This made Maman and Lili laugh hysterically.

Baba Nourie finally found a Rabbi to slaughter the bird the next day to avoid the hassle and the mess the bird made in the house. The family managed to forget about the bird's death the minute they took the first bites of the delicious, hot turkey meat.

Maman cooked, cleaned, and washed nonstop with a thankful heart. She managed to take care of several awful sicknesses that resulted from the lack of sanitation in the water and outside sewer system. The worst memory was when Davood had a very high fever along with scary hallucinations. He kept kicking his legs and moved his arms in various directions and whispered nonsense most of the night in his bed. Two nights of restlessness and applying old remedies did not help. Finally, Davood was rushed to a nearby hospital, where he was diagnosed with an unusual virus that affected his brain, causing the nonstop hallucinations. The doctors prescribed strong medication to lower the fever. Thankfully, Davood got over the sickness after a couple of weeks of Maman's tender loving care and plenty of prayers. Maman had experienced yet another near-death drama in her life. This made her faith stronger than ever, unlike other parents who sometimes blamed God for family disasters.

One of the worst memories from this time period was when a strong earthquake struck that part of Iran. It was a hot summer night when "The Mansion" started to shake. Baba Nourie woke up first and alerted the family frantically. Maman woke up with terror. The children did not awaken, even with the loud sounds of their parents. There was no time to waste, so Baba Nourie asked his wife to go out to the flat field immediately. He then grabbed each child by his or her shoulders and literally threw them off the balcony one by one, with each landing on the soft weedy garden plants. Amazingly, everyone woke up with no broken bones, but felt terrified because they did not know what was going on.

"GET OUT!" Baba Nourie demanded with a loud scream. "Go to the open field immediately and join your mother," he continued yelling. Giti was a great help, holding Lili and pushing her siblings toward the field. A crying Maman reached out to her children and hugged them all at the same time. The ground continued shaking and the crying of the many neighboring families huddled together in the wide open field intensified with each aftershock. The nightmare slowly ended after several hours, and everyone woke up to the early rays of sunshine covering the field. They all thanked God, many praising

Allah and a few praising *Hashem* [Hebrew for "The Name"—a polite way of saying God]. All the neighbors started hugging each other while they were headed back to their houses.

The damage was minor in the Arianah area, while major devastation occurred on the other side of the city and outskirt areas, with many dead and injured. The family cleaned up the scattered pots and pans strewn about "The Mansion" and took long naps without feeling hunger or thirst.

CHAPTER TEN

THE HASSAN-ABAD HOUSE

AFTER LIVING IN "THE ARIANA MANSION" for several years, Baba Nourie's business with his brother was booming and a side job as a furniture cleaner yielded enough money to purchase a house close to the business. The neighborhood was a mixture of Muslims and Armenian Christians. It looked like an ideal international community where there were no people with hate-filled looks and insulting comments. All the families enjoyed looking outside, and observing the gathering of their children playing together.

The new house was located in a small alley, which was connected to a larger alley with some houses made of mud and some made of fancy stone and marble. This house, located in Hassan Abad, was within walking distance of the dry cleaning business.

The family quickly moved in and distributed the furniture throughout several small rooms. The yard was a completely square shape with a perfectly rectangular Hoze [a small decorative pond] in the center. Baba Nourie arranged several potted plants around the Hoze to make his wife happy, since she missed the small gardens at "The Arianah Mansion." He also added several goldfish in the Hoze to make it look like another mansion.

The scariest part of the house was the bathroom located in the far corner. It was made of very old stones with black mud between them. Spiderwebs formed the wallpaper all around the bathroom with many baby spiders waiting to be

born. In the center was a fairly large hole. There were two small oval-shaped areas on the opposite sides of the hole for squatting. The Aftabeh [a tall, plastic water container for washing] looked like a small monster from another planet ready to attack, since there was only one dim lightbulb illuminating the small room. The children tried to hold their bladders and bowels as long as they could in order not to face the monster in the dark with its baby creatures hanging on the walls. Lili would cry every time she came out of the bathroom.

Maman was energetic doing all the chores. One day Baba Nourie brought one of the best gifts that only a rich Iranian could have—a refrigerator! Everyone was so happy to have such a fancy thing in their home. Lili screamed, "We are rich, we are rich," while everyone stared at the new arrival as if a new baby had been born. Maman could now boast in front of the neighbors like a rich woman, but she really did not mean it. Instead, her heart was inclined to God, thanking him for these material things. The refrigerator was not a new one, but was second-hand with two big problems: a malfunctioning freezer that generated very thick, bulky ice, and a metallic door handle that gave a mild electric shock. Every time someone touched the door to open it, they received a jolt and screamed. Sometimes the children used a belt carefully placed around the door handle to yank it open. Lili would always beg tearfully for someone to open the refrigerator door for her. The boys made a big game out of this malfunctioning refrigerator as if it were an alien from outer space trying to kill the females. Kamran was amused by the jolts more than his brothers and kept grabbing the handle for several minutes while making his entire body shake and letting out screeching screams. Davood and Moris were entertained, laughing while watching Kamran. Lili used to cry out loud, running away every time her brother became involved in this silly game.

CHAPTER ELEVEN

MICKEY MOUSE AND NO MORE SOFREH!

ONE SABBATH NIGHT, Maman prepared a delicious dinner and served it with Sabzee [assorted green herbs, red radishes, and chunks of feta cheese]. Everyone helped place the dishes and utensils on the Sofreh [a rectangular or circular Persian-decorated cloth placed on the floor]. Baba Nourie brought two Sabbath candles and placed them on the brass-plated candle holder. He then asked everyone to remain sitting around the Sofreh and wait for great news after Maman finished the prayers for the candles and the Sabbath bread.

The children obeyed and patiently waited for the news. Baba Nourie recited the Hebrew prayer for the bread, which involved breaking the bread into small pieces and rubbing them with salt, then placing them on his plate and giving them to everyone to eat.

"Amen," all the kids said at the same time while they ate their salty bread pieces. "What is the big news now?" the kids asked.

"This is not just big news, it is the biggest news!" Baba Nourie said.

"Ahh…" all the kids said at the same time.

"Another baby. We know! We are used to this kind of surprise by now," Giti announced.

"No, you silly kids," Baba Nourie replied, laughing.

"Let me start it with a question," he continued. "What are the two main things that make an Iranian family rich?"

"But we are rich now," Lili interrupted quickly. "We have a refrigerator," she said, pointing to the electrical alien.

"That is a half right answer to my question," Baba Nourie replied with a smile to his smart daughter.

But before he continued, the rest of the kids all screamed exactly the same thing: "A television?"

"Yep. A great, working, used TV! But I would say a good-deal TV," Baba Nourie said proudly.

"When…when…when will we have it? When?" all the

kids screamed while jumping up and down and running around like lost chickens. Maman started to laugh at her children acting silly with their mouths full.

"Be careful, kids, you still have food in your mouths!" Maman said while still laughing. It was a joyful memory for Maman.

Thank you God for bringing another blessing to this family, Maman whispered in her heart.

So the traditional imaginary rich Iranian family waited for days impatiently until another electrical alien invaded their home, but this time there was neither thick ice nor an electricity-jolting handle. Davood helped put the long-rod antenna on the flat mud roof and the rest of the family stared at the clock impatiently until six o'clock when the TV programs would start to broadcast. Davood turned on the TV about ten minutes before six to make sure it was working. Everyone stared in awe at the screen filled with black and white fuzz. Even Maman was distracted from performing her daily chores for a while.

The fuzzy scene finally cleared and a picture of the Shah of Iran with an Iranian flag in the background appeared along with the sounds of the Iranian national anthem.

"WOW!" shouted everyone at the same time.

There were several local programs, short news, Persian and Indian movies, but the family's favorite programs were the commercials and the Mickey Mouse cartoons.

The commercial announcements were broadcast in a fifteen-minute block of time after every couple of hours of main programing. This was a special time for the family to laugh and enjoy their favorite TV programs.

The black-and-white, English-language Mickey Mouse cartoons were very popular in Iran. Even though these cartoons were repeated many times, the family never got tired of watching them.

How was it possible, everyone wondered, that these drawings could move and talk?

Every night the children gathered around the TV and watched the programs until nine o'clock when the broadcasts ended. The blessing of having a TV and watching family programs together meant a lot to Maman.

Several months later, Baba Nourie brought home yet another surprise—a round dining table with chairs. This was the first time ever that the family could eat around the table instead of a traditional Sofreh.

"Now you don't have to bend over so many times and clean up after these messy kids around the Sofreh," Baba Nourie told Maman. He received a big kiss from Maman.

The dry cleaning business was doing well and Baba Nourie could afford to buy more second-hand household furniture, perhaps spending a little too much, but it was worth seeing his happy family together.

After more than a year of being in partnership with his brother Faze-Allah, the relationship went sour over the shared business expenses.

"So what are you going to do?" asked Maman, sounding worried.

"Don't know yet," Baba Nourie replied. "My brother cannot catch up with the expensive repairs, plus the lack of customers nowadays," he continued. "Perhaps I should quit this job and start looking for odd jobs again." He sighed.

"Can you hang in there for a while before making a major decision?" Maman suggested.

"I'll talk with Faze-Allah and come up with a solution," Baba Nourie replied with some confidence. He left the house with an incomplete and uncertain hope for the near future.

"My brother and I will be holding on to the business together for now," Baba Nourie announced after he came home very late.

Maman was already tucked in bed but fully awake, waiting for her husband's arrival.

"Let's just enjoy what we have now and wait for God's will," Baba Nourie said quietly while tucking himself in bed next to Maman.

"Shab-beh-Khayre [goodnight]," they whispered to each other.

Several months passed with lots of cooking, eating, Mickey Mouse cartoons and Indian movies, and joyful moments until, one day, Baba Nourie told his wife that the dry cleaning business was on the verge of collapse.

"We have to cut back on everything," Baba Nourie told Maman. For Maman, these were just more days of poverty, which everyone had become accustomed to. The kids had already realized that things did not seem right. They were no longer eating two or three meals a day. The refrigerator was empty and had been turned off, along with the TV, for several days to save electricity.

Many times Maman had only bread and halvah [a sweet paste of butter, sugar and flour] or plain yogurt as the one meal of the day. One hot summer night, the family slept on the flat roof since there was no air conditioning in the house. The family had gone to bed hungry for many nights, but that did not kill Maman's spirit for loving God and she never stopped her daily Khodar Rah Shokr. On that hot summer night, Maman brought a huge tray filled with old bread crumbs and asked her children to gather round and challenged them to a contest to see who could eat the fastest. The kids rushed over, grabbed as many of the crumbs as they could reach, and quickly ate them until the tray was cleaned off. Once again, everyone went to bed hungry, but this night at least they had some bread crumbs in their stomachs.

After the collapse of the dry cleaning business, Baba Nourie was hardly home since he was doing many odd jobs to keep up with the family's basic needs. Maman never lost hope and faith in God, who had provided many blessings for the family so far. She was confident that God would provide again in the future. She was amazed at her children's contentment with their lives. They never stopped playing joyfully with each other despite the circumstances.

One night Giti overheard a conversation between Maman and Baba Nourie. She heard something about electric and water bills, and dreaded words that Giti did not want to hear again—moving out.

"Are we poor again, Maman Joon?" Giti asked the next morning, making sure that her siblings did not hear her.

"Well…yes and no, Giti Joon," Maman replied with a confidence that her grown-up daughter would understand. "Right now there is no steady income, as you know," Maman continued. "So we have to wait patiently and see what God has in store for us next."

"Can we sell our TV and refrigerator?" Giti suggested. "That way you guys can pay some of the bills."

"Bills?" Maman interrupted Giti. "Where did you hear that?" Maman continued.

"Well, I overheard that Baba Nourie cannot pay the water bill and the other bills. I don't know," Giti replied with a stutter while shrugging her shoulders.

"Don't worry about a thing, dear, things will be better soon," Maman assured Giti.

But things did not get better anytime soon.

Maman heard some men outside the door announcing that the water must be shut off. She begged them to wait for several minutes so she could bring some buckets to fill with drinking water before they shut off the main water pipe. They agreed and the family had enough water in the buckets for several days.

The family stopped watching TV and turning lights on, fearing that the electricity would be shut off next. It didn't happen.

After several weeks of struggling, Baba Nourie brought fairly good news to the family. He told everyone that one of his odd jobs was helping one of his Muslim friends who was a lawyer. To Maman this was a blessing, like when God had blessed Hagar [a non-Jewish woman] with her son Ishmael, who was blessed by God to create a great nation. Sometimes Maman thought, *What if all Iranian Muslims read this portion of Torah* [Hebrew for The Five Books of Moses in God's Word]*, which is also in their Holy Quran? Then they might get along with all non-Muslims.*

The extra income helped restore the water and brought food to the table. This time the chicken-feet soup tasted like they were biting into a juicy lamb chunk! The kids never complained again as they had before about any parts of the chicken in the soup.

Not only did God give back some of the material

things, he also provided more great news—Maman was pregnant again!

CHAPTER TWELVE

BIRTH OF MISHEL

NEARING HER MID-FORTIES, Maman looked so young, beautiful, and full of energy. However, one day she felt quite sick. She wanted to throw up but was too weak. The best medicine for her was her children gathering around and reassuring her of their love. They rubbed a wet washcloth on her face, saying, *"Maman Joon, Maman Joon* [Dear Mama]."

"Is Maman dying?" Lili asked everyone in a trembling voice. Baba Nourie took his wife and rushed her to the nearest clinic. No one could go to sleep, thinking Baba Nourie might come back alone with awful news.

Giti's head was filled with the painful memories of her first baby brother. This time she thought Baba Nourie would come back without her mother. That thought evaporated quickly since she could not bear not having Maman around. She needed some assurance and some hope. She reached out to her baby sister Lili and gave her a hug and some kisses. That was enough assurance and hope for Giti. The boys asked their sisters if Maman was going to be alright, but they received no answer, just sad looks.

"I heard some boys from our neighborhood saying that fever can kill people," Kamran said, sounding scared. That did not help the other boys. Giti started to worry more since she too had recently heard about people getting sick with a high fever and dying. She also heard there was a deadly disease going around that caused an unusual fever, but she didn't show her worries to her siblings and acted like their mother by reassuring them that Maman would be fine.

"We have to get some sleep and dream of happy and funny memories," Giti told her siblings in a motherly tone. They all agreed with fake smiles and slept for a couple of hours until they heard footsteps by the door. They got up with racing heartbeats, terrified. But the terror turned into great relief.

Baba Nourie happily announced that their mother was having another baby. The children screamed with happiness, yet were puzzled at the same time.

"How could Maman be carrying another baby at this age?" the children exclaimed. "She is too old!"

"And why was she having a fever?" Giti asked curiously.

"Look kids, your mother was sick due to a combination of a common cold and some pregnancy sickness," Baba Nourie said.

All the children reached out to Maman and had a group hug. They asked her to rest until the fever was gone. "We don't want the baby to get sick too," the children said compassionately.

For the next several months, Maman went through episodes of high fever and severe headaches.

Perhaps this will be the last pregnancy for me, she thought while resting in bed. But she happily waited until the delivery day.

The baby boy Mishel came out right on time with no complications. He had a chubby round face with dark brown eyes and lots of black hair. The minute baby Mishel came home, everyone began fighting over him. He was showered with constant kisses, even when attached to Maman's breasts! Everyone forgot about the previous "miracle" [the black-and-white TV] and paid a great deal of attention to both Maman and her nursing baby. The children also enjoyed watching Maman, who would often look skyward, thanking God constantly. The love of God was always at the center of her growing family circle.

Baby Mishel's early years were filled with joy and royal treatment as if he were a prince. The expression, *Ghorboonet Beram* [I die for you], was constantly heard around the child, offering deep love from the family members. Living in the Hassan-Abad house was glorious after Mishel's arrival. The siblings were so delighted to take care of Mishel that they forgot the fear of the "dungeon bathroom!"

Mishel became the center of attention in the family. The best memory for Maman was when all the children sat around her in a circle while she was nursing Mishel. The boys and Lili waited impatiently and kept inching closer to Maman in order to grab the baby when he was finished nursing. Giti, who was standing behind the circle, acted like a commander-in-chief. She assigned who got the baby first and for how long! Everyone had a fair share in holding and kissing Mishel at the end. This royal treatment would not end until "the prince" fell asleep! Even then there was another game going on—staring at the sleeping prince.

Despite all of the constant loving care around the baby, Giti started to worry about her baby brother's safety the most, especially around the yard when Mishel started to crawl and walk. The Hoze, a small fish pond in the middle of the yard with brick plant pots situated on its edge, the steps with broken bricks leading to the dungeon [toilet], and several suspicious holes in the corners of the yard close to the dungeon were all potentially dangerous. Many times Giti noticed crawling creatures coming out of the holes, going back and forth. The big creatures looked like mice, but they didn't look like ordinary mice. They were much fatter with long tails and scary paws with long nails. The other creatures were the ones Baba Nourie warned everyone to stay away from—Hezar-Pa [scorpions]—which were common in that part of Tehran. Every time Giti announced the Hezar-Pa warnings, all the kids put cotton balls in their ears and put on heavy socks before going to bed, fearing that the creatures would crawl into their ears or bite their toes. Kamran was the only one who wasn't scared. He often took the opportunity to scare the rest, especially Lili, by teasing them—"What if a Hezar-Pa crawls into your nose!" Everyone ignored Kamran and tried to fall asleep.

One day Maman heard from the neighbors that there was a spread of a disease with very high fever, similar to the bubonic plague caused by rats. That confirmed the rumor Giti and Kamran had heard before. Maman warned and begged her husband to do something about those holes full of rats. Baba Nourie did not waste time and asked everyone to stay inside the rooms with the windows closed. The kids did not obey fully. Baby Mishel was fast asleep next to Maman, and the kids huddled around a closed window overlooking the yard. The window panes were small and dirty so there was not enough clear glass to see through. Giti reached out and opened the window slowly to avoid the squeaking noise from the rusty hinges. Lili was trembling and fearful while holding on to Giti's arms, but the boys looked excited and curious about what would happen next.

Now they could see the corner of the yard where Baba Nourie was doing something strange. Next to him was the water hose, a pair of long tongs, a small can of gasoline, and a box of matches.

"Why would he need all these things to kill the creatures?" Lili quietly asked Giti with a trembling voice. "I thought you just need a hammer to kill the creatures or you step on them."

Before Giti answered her scared sister, Baba Nourie started his mysterious performance. He inserted the hose in the biggest hole in the ground and turned on the faucet fully. He waited for several minutes and then turned the water off.

To everybody's amazement a small parade of soaked rats came out of the hole slowly, one by one, with no energy to run. The next step was the scariest of all. Baba Nourie quickly grabbed the wet rats one by one with the tongs, spraying some gasoline on them, and then lighting them with matches.

Lili immediately turned around and hugged Giti to avoid the awful rat executions, while the boys were amazed by them.

Giti closed the window and asked everyone to stop watching the awful rat killing in the yard. They all felt guilty about the rats and at the same time were disappointed in their father's cruelty.

Baba Nourie spent several hours in the yard making sure all the rats were exterminated, and then he trashed the completely charred bodies. He closed the holes with some dirt and rocks. After washing his hands with soap and hot water for several minutes, he came in to the room to an unhappy crowd.

"Why did you kill them like that?" Giti asked Baba Nourie on behalf of her siblings.

"Burning the deadly microbes in these rats is the only way to make sure my entire family is safe," Baba Nourie announced, sounding worn-out. "Now it's safe to go in the yard if you want."

They all went out to play together for several hours to be distracted from what happened in the yard. The thought of food did not cross their minds for several hours after the rat-burning event.

Maman was very thankful to her husband for getting rid of the rats, and hoped that she would never see another one in the yard. She asked everyone to be cautious when they were in the yard or going to the dungeon.

Several weeks later, Baba Nourie told his wife some good news about the dry cleaning business. He and his brother Faze-Allah made peace and were successful in reviving the business. It was a slow revival but better than total bankruptcy, thanks to some personal loans Faze-Allah had been able to get from some friends.

Once again Baba Nourie thanked God for the blessings of not losing the house and being able to stay in the dry cleaning business. And what a blessed coincidence: It all happened right after Yom Kippur, the day of atonement when the Jews fast, read Torah and pray for a whole day, requesting God to forgive their sins. But the blessings didn't stop there. The joy of fasting and Jewish togetherness during Yom Kippur was a divine blessing for the Jews, since it made them stop for one day to remember their Creator and thank Him through prayers. Maman described this Jewish togetherness as "glue" that bonded all the Jews together and made the survival of the Jewish nation possible throughout the years.

Mishel was nearly three years old when Baba Nourie brought the good news that he was earning enough money from both the dry cleaning business and his side jobs to pay the bills. It was clearly the result of Maman quoting the Torah's writings about God's promises. After years of poverty, hunger, homelessness, atrocities against the Jews, and above all, the pain of losing their firstborn son, God gave Baba Nourie enough blessings so that he could present his family with a house of their own.

"You mean we actually would buy a house and not rent one?" Maman asked her husband.

"Yes!" Baba Nourie replied with great joy.

CHAPTER THIRTEEN

THE JAMSHID-ABAD HOUSE AND THE END OF THE "DUNGEON"

"A HOUSE WITH A HOT SHOWER and a safe bathroom?" the children cried out loudly. It was a two-story house with a yard and a small basement. Baba Nourie managed to buy new furniture and new pots and pans. The house was in a clean alley with decent-looking adjacent houses, with trees in the yards that gave plenty of shade. Many houses had multiple stories with decorative balconies covered with rose flowers. The new family house had a huge blue metallic gate leading to a square yard, with plenty of space to build vegetable and herb gardens. On the right side of the yard there were several steps leading to the first and second floors. Baba Nourie decided to move the family to the second floor and rent the first floor to another family in the future. Everyone happily agreed. Baba Nourie was especially amazed to see a small basement underneath the first floor, which had been built for storage, but he had another plan for it—raising pigeons.

"Pigeons?" Maman exclaimed with surprise when her husband told her about his plan.

"My father and I used to raise lots of them in our small backyard when I was young," Baba Nourie replied.

"For what reason?" Maman asked.

"To eat, what else?!" Baba Nourie said, laughing.

"Shhh…don't you say a word about this to the kids, at least not yet," Maman replied quietly. The children, especially Lili, were still sensitive to killing animals. Baba Nourie agreed and called the children to go upstairs and check the rooms. As soon as they opened the door to the second floor, they were all amazed to see two huge rooms: a kitchen, a bathroom, and a balcony overlooking the alley.

"A bathroom built here next to the kitchen?" Lili screamed.

"Yep," Kamran replied, "and you don't have to worry about any creatures in a dungeon anymore."

The children stayed on the balcony while their parents were checking out the rest of the floor.

While everyone was busy unpacking, Maman stopped for a moment and looked at her joyful family. *How could it be?* she thought to herself. *My grownup children, except Mishel, are still playing, laughing, teasing, and loving each other as if they never grew up.* Many memories raced through her mind—the memories of their wedding, the births of the children, poverty, political unrest, and the great tragedy of losing her first son. She looked up and thanked God for His promises and blessings throughout those years.

Maman came out of the frozen moment when she heard Lili running around with excitement, but she went back again to another daydream as soon as her last son, Mishel, walked in the room and quickly passed by her with a happy dance.

Oh…yeah…and my prince son, Mishel, she thought happily, since he was being showered with kisses from everyone every time his siblings got a chance to catch the prince.

Maman quickly realized that those years of raising her kids had never blocked even one moment from that awful tragedy of losing her first son, Moris. Part of her heart was broken forever. She thanked God again for His unfailing love that helped her to get through the tragedy.

Too Many Goodbyes

Giti was the first one to leave the nest. It was a bittersweet goodbye since she had to go to Israel to be with her husband, who had immigrated years earlier.

Maman was so thrilled to see her precious helper, Giti, move overseas to meet her pre-arranged husband-to-be. Even though Giti decided to reside in Israel, Maman's heart did not want to surrender to the warning from their relatives living in Israel, telling the rest of the family to come live there as well.

At the airport, Maman looked at Giti tearfully and thanked her for all the wonderful help for many years. Baba Nourie and all the siblings hugged and kissed Giti goodbye. As Giti was going through the checkpoints, Maman waved and said a prayer for a safe trip. There were tough times ahead of Giti—facing political instability in Israel and the new life she was about to begin. But Giti was tough, a strong tomboy, and determined. Giti disappeared into the crowd of passengers waiting to board an Israeli plane.

Maman and her family quickly went outside the airport to a designated fenced-in area where they could see the plane in the distance and the line of passengers stepping onto the plane. There were plenty of heavily-armed guards in the area to protect the plane and the passengers. Iran was the only country in the Middle East to have a direct flight from Tehran to Tel-Aviv—the Israeli capital at that time. It was a special privilege for the Iranian Jews to have the freedom to travel directly to Israel.

While the plane flew over their heads and disappeared into the thin clouds, Maman's heart raced and her mind was flooded with memories. She became light-headed since there were so many memories to focus on.

Everyone waved to the plane in the sky and loudly said, "Goodbye, Giti Joon!"

On the way back home, Maman dreaded yet another goodbye—Kamran would be the next to leave home.

Within several months of the first goodbye, Kamran graduated from high school and was the second one to fly out of the nest, not just a few miles away from home, but several thousand miles to America.

"I want to pursue a degree in general studies in America," Kamran exclaimed, even though his heart desired to become a professional soccer player.

There were only a handful of Iranian universities and

colleges to accommodate thousands of high school graduates, therefore, many students looked into continuing their education in America. Since Iran had a stable relationship with America, there was a huge demand from the young Iranian students to get accepted into American colleges—any college. The business of getting acceptance letters from American colleges was booming in Iran!

Kamran was so excited to leave and start his own life in a foreign land with bright sunshine, pretty blond-haired and blue-eyed girls, and rich people who had never experienced hunger and poverty. This was the way the majority of the young Iranian generation thought of America, since the American movies and TV shows fooled the naïve Iranian boys and girls at that time.

Despite this imagined view of America, Kamran had something else in mind—becoming a famous soccer player. After all, it was encoded in his DNA when he was formed in his mother's womb!

Once again there was a gathering at the airport to say goodbye to another bird leaving the nest. Maman reached out to Kamran with tears in her eyes and showered him with kisses and hugs.

"You'd better stop goofing off playing soccer all the time and start focusing on your education," Maman demanded. Kamran nodded while crying hard. Everyone else gave Kamran big hugs and kisses and shed some tears as he was disappearing into the crowd that was heading toward the boarding entrance.

"Will there be any other goodbyes anytime soon?" Maman asked her husband sarcastically. "What is this? One moment you see your kids around the Korsi huddling and begging for food, and the next moment you see them flying out of the country in giant airplanes!"

Baba Nourie was speechless when he heard his wife's comments. His mind was also flooded with memories of raising Kamran. He was thankful and proud to see Kamran grow up and leave the nest, despite the stress of the high cost of these overseas travels and education.

The rest of the siblings were still around since Davood was going to a Jewish vocational school and Moris was pursuing his degree in chemistry at an Iranian university. Maman and Baba Nourie never forgot the cheerful moment when Moris announced his acceptance to a well-known university in Tehran, since only a handful of graduates with high scores could be admitted. Maman was confident that this was an answer to her prayer to God to avoid another long distance goodbye.

Lili and Mishel were still in school, trying to graduate. Lili graduated successfully, but God had a different plan for Mishel when he reached seventeen years of age.

Within a year, the family received many letters and expensive phone calls from Giti and Kamran from overseas. There were many sweet short phone conversations. Maman tried to focus on the funny ones, such as Kamran being as famous as the internationally known Brazilian soccer player, Pelé, at his college, and the other phone call admitting that America was not even close to what those stupid TV programs and movies presented in Iran!

Kamran was also encouraging Moris to come to America to continue his graduate studies. He didn't want to admit his loneliness in America, and that he wanted to have his brother Moris near him. But he couldn't fool Maman since she already knew Kamran's heart's desire. She started praying much harder this time not to lose her son Moris.

"But we have to let go of them, sooner or later," Baba Nourie told his crying wife.

"I cannot afford the absence of our Moris," Maman replied.

"You want him to stay with us for the rest of his life?" Baba Nourie replied with a hint of sarcasm.

"I tell you what," Baba Nourie suggested, "you can go with Moris to Israel, have a visit with Giti and our relatives who are citizens now, and then let Moris fly to America from there. Isn't that a good plan?"

"Can we really afford another expense for Moris' travel overseas?" Maman asked worriedly.

"Well, you remember that I saved up some money and some Persian carpets I earned by bartering with some rich families I worked for?" Baba Nourie replied. "Don't worry. I can come up with the money. I just want you to spend some time with our son and the other family members overseas. You deserve it."

Another goodbye ceremony occurred at the airport, but this time Baba Nourie was the one with the most tears. He was saying goodbye to Moris and his wife at the same time. "Good thing that Hamsareh-Azizam [my dear wife] will come back," Baba Nourie said.

Both Maman and her son Moris had a great reunion with Giti and Baba Nourie's sisters and their families who had resided in Israel since many years ago. The relatives welcomed Maman and her son, but at the same time they warned Maman about the deteriorating political situation in Iran and the fragile freedom of the Iranian Jews.

"But the Shah of Iran is wonderful to the Jews and has a good relationship with Israel," Maman kept replying to most of the relatives who were warning her about their prediction of the collapse of the Iranian government in the near future.

"Why wait any longer?" the relatives kept warning Maman. "You know that we hear some reliable news here in Israel about the possible revolution in Iran, so all of you must think of leaving Iran and immigrating to Israel while the traveling is still easy. The only safe place for all the Jews to live is Israel as God promised, and you should stay and ask the rest of the family to travel soon while there is freedom to travel abroad."

"No, things are well in Iran and we have finally made a good life after going through years of hardship and agony," Maman said with confidence.

"The Shah of Iran will not live forever, but the fanatic Muslims will," one of the relatives shouted.

This hit Maman's heart very hard even though there was

some truth to these warnings. She remembered the awful anti-Jewish words from some fanatic Muslims during the Shah's regime. There was always the smell of hatred in the air whenever some news media talked about Israeli conflicts with her Arab neighbors, or even during the 1972 Munich Olympic Games where the death of many Israeli athletes created a joyful celebration in many parts of Iran.

She even thought of a day when her young second Moris was walking along in a park looking for water, but he could not find the water fountain. He politely asked a couple of Muslim men if they could show him where it was. The men curiously asked his name and as soon as they heard the name Moris, which was a typical Jewish name, they realized that the boy was a Joohood [filthy Jew]. They shouted at Moris with hatred-filled faces, "If we knew you were a Joohood, we would never have showed you the drinking fountain!" The painful words that Moris shared with Maman upon his return were still vivid in her mind. Maman never forgot the sight of her trembling, confused son that day.

"Ok…ok…we'll see," Maman replied to the relative, trying to end the tiresome conversation and forget the unwanted memories.

I think these relatives are completely wrong, Maman thought while she was leaving their house and heading to the airport for a lonely goodbye with her precious son.

The Israeli airport was crowded with many international travelers. The security soldiers were seen everywhere. There was no time for a long talk and goodbye since there was a lengthy security procedure to be completed before boarding any plane.

By the grace of God, Maman showed an amazing strength and showed no tears when she said goodbye to Moris.

"Khoda Negahdaret Basheh [May God protect you]," Maman whispered in Moris' ears while kissing him goodbye. Moris kissed Maman's cheeks several times, looked into her eyes and tearfully pleaded with Maman not to worry about him too much.

"Don't worry, Moris Joon, I promise," Maman replied, blinking back tears.

As Moris was on the escalator going up toward the heavily-armed security area on the second floor, he looked down and saw Maman smiling and waving with kisses toward him. He felt better about Maman's promise and was very confident she would be fine. He was wrong.

Moris safely traveled to America and joined Kamran in Ohio. After several months, Moris went to a college near where Kamran lived to pursue his chemistry degree. He was constantly in touch with Maman to make sure everybody in the family was safe, due to the disturbing news coming from Iran. He promised to come home for a visit while there was still freedom to travel.

CHAPTER FOURTEEN

THE RELATIVES WERE RIGHT—CHAOS AND ESCAPING IRAN

THE ECHO OF "COME TO ISRAEL" became more realistic every day. It was in late 1976 that the situation in Iran started deteriorating rapidly. Maman started to panic. Moris came home from America for a visit during summer vacation, but the visit had lasted less than a month when the news of the Shah of Iran's collapsing government became widespread.

Moris arrived in Tehran where there was not much political chaos, but he could sense that the news he heard in America could become more realistic soon. The TV news showed awful pictures of dead and injured people through violence caused by some anti-Iranians—as the media claimed—in many cities, but they reassured people that the Shah would stay, and life would go on as usual.

Less than two weeks into Moris' stay, rumors of a huge revolution started to spread everywhere in Tehran. It wasn't only the fear of being a Jew in Iran that terrified Maman, but living in Iran became unsafe, for Jews or non-Jews. Many people rushed to the stores to stock up on basic needs at any cost, and many started to pack and head to the airport.

Maman begged Moris to leave Iran immediately since the airport was in chaos with people desperately trying to flee Iran. Baba Nourie and Maman packed all of Moris' belongings into a big suitcase and hurried to the airport in a taxi. The line of weary travelers could be seen coming out of the airport building as their loud screams to get on a flight, ANY FLIGHT, could be heard while they were driving up to the building.

Maman begged the airport workers behind the luggage counter to take Moris' suitcase and put it and her son on the flight to Germany with a connection to New York. They refused. The begging cries of Maman did nothing until Baba Nourie came to the rescue with a bunch of colorful money in his hand. The bribe worked. The goodbyes were very quick and Moris disappeared into the noisy, shoving crowd toward the main gate to the airplane where he was whisked away.

Moris called Maman to inform her of his safe return to America. He and Kamran, along with other Iranian friends, were constantly on the watch for political developments in Iran.

"Will there be any revolution in Iran? And if so, how will we be able to visit our family again?" Moris asked Kamran worriedly.

"I don't know, but the news seems bad and something drastic could happen anytime," Kamran replied.

For the next several months, the news of a possible revolution in Iran was broadcast worldwide. The TV news programs constantly showed rioting in various cities in Iran. Moris had to be positive, since he was close to his graduation. Thankfully, the phone communications between America and Iran were still working. Whenever Moris or Kamran made a phone call, they tried to avoid talking about any political subjects since they heard many rumors of phone tapping by the Iranian secret services.

"Things are very normal here, thanks to the Shah of Iran," Maman said to Moris on the phone.

"Are you thinking about Eretz?" Moris said carefully.

Eretz was a secret word that meant "the land" in Hebrew, referring to Israel.

"Yes," Maman said, obviously worried. She changed the subject immediately and asked how Moris' personal life was, besides studying hard.

Moris was delighted to announce the news that he'd met an American girl who was also a student at the same college.

"We've been seeing each other for several months now and I am going to ask her to marry me!" Moris said excitedly.

"Is she Jewish?" Maman interrupted immediately.

"I know, Maman Joon, I promised to marry a Jewish woman to keep the Jewish identity in our future generations," Moris replied, "but I am hoping to have your blessing on this marriage."

"She is a very Godly Christian girl and best of all, she is a great cook!" Moris continued.

"At least have a Jewish marriage ceremony," Maman told him.

"Absolutely!" Moris replied happily.

"Mobarak-Basheh [congratulations] and kiss your future wife for us," Maman replied.

The chaotic political situation in many cities was getting worse, and soon Tehran, the capital, was the next target. The first thing that came to Maman's mind was to hide her seventeen-year-old son Mishel so that he could avoid being drafted by the Iranian military into mandatory service.

"We have to send Mishel out of the country soon," Baba Nourie suggested firmly.

"We cannot just buy a plane ticket and fly him out of Iran. We ought to do something quickly," Maman replied in tears.

"Let me contact some of my friends who might be able to help us," Baba Nourie replied. He asked Maman to stay home and rest until he came up with a viable solution. But Maman was restless and started to pace the room while she was praying. She begged God to show mercy for Mishel's safety. She thought about a portion of Torah referring to the chapter in Exodus where God miraculously freed the Israelites from slavery and helped them exit Egypt.

"Now this could be the time that God performs a miracle for my son to exit Iran safely," Maman prayed.

Baba Nourie finally managed to contact several trustworthy Muslim friends who were helping people escape the country through various neighboring borders.

"This is a dangerous and expensive solution," Baba Nourie told Maman, "but this is the only feasible solution for our son to get out."

With a heavy heart, Maman agreed.

Baba Nourie had already contacted his friends for the escape instructions. He was asked to get Mishel ready and wait outside the house at two o'clock the next morning. The escape plan was so quick that there was no time for Maman and her husband to think twice.

Maman begged her husband for more details about the plan.

"They will drive Mishel to the Iran-Turkey border and he will stay in some safe border towns until he is able to fly out to Israel," Baba Nourie informed her.

Mishel had all the information on the plan, especially the names of the contact people who would help him reach the Israeli embassy to fly to Israel.

Mishel was very depressed and confused, but he knew the reality of the situation very well. So he pretended to be strong and promised Maman he would see her again in Israel.

At about two o'clock in the morning, there was a knock on the door. Maman was already awake, too upset to sleep. She grabbed a siddur [Hebrew prayer book] and a glass of water to pour behind Mishel, symbolizing safe travel and being hopeful for a reunion. A car with three men in it was parked near the house, and without making any noise, they signaled a quick move for Mishel to slide into the vehicle. Then they disappeared into the dark of night, and there was nothing left for Maman to do except beg God to be with her son all the way through this unknown journey.

The news of many Iranians, Jews and non-Jews, fleeing Iran was broadcast worldwide. Many were arrested and others died trying to escape through the various borders. Maman's heart was so saddened that she cried daily, sometimes hitting her head with her hands, symbolizing the deep worry about what might happen to her young son. The fear and anxiety of losing another son was a threat to Maman's survival. Her blood pressure rose, severe headaches began, and blood tests revealed health problems. Maman's blood glucose levels especially worried Baba Nourie.

CHAPTER FIFTEEN

MIRACLES, A HELLISH ESCAPE, AND PAKISTANI ANGELS!

AFTER SEVERAL DAYS of agonized waiting and prayers, Baba Nourie received the miraculous news from his friends that Mishel had made it through the border safely and was now traveling to Israel through Turkey!

The news gave Maman new life, and the rest of the family members came out of their state of deep sadness upon hearing the news.

Mishel arrived in Israel on a flight from Turkey to find his sister Giti waiting for him. She had already become an Israeli citizen and had prepared a new life for her little brother. She welcomed Mishel into her home as a member of her own family.

The good news of Mishel's arrival in Israel was another miracle from God to Maman. However, it was too late to repair the physical damage done to her body. She developed many symptoms of diabetes, but she did not pay attention to them and instead focused her heart, mind, and soul on Mishel's safety.

Due to the political instability and the news of the human smugglers who were paid by many Iranian citizens to help them flee the country, the government imposed strict guidelines for overseas travels and placed heavy secret police forces at the borders. Women were allowed to travel abroad only for medical reasons under their husbands' or relatives' consent. Maman took this opportunity and contacted her mother, Nana, and suggested flying to Switzerland for medical reasons. She would then travel on to Israel to join their other family members. Nana gladly agreed.

Baba Nourie had to sign a consent agreement and use his house as collateral to ensure the return of his wife and Nana, otherwise the house would be confiscated. Baba Nourie didn't hesitate for a moment.

Nana and Maman traveled to Switzerland with temporary visas based upon medical needs. The American embassy was flooded with Iranian Jews applying for asylum to Israel since the Israeli government welcomed Jews from around the world to reside there. After several weeks stay in Switzerland, both Maman and Nana received their asylum visas and flew safely to Israel.

The gates of Heaven opened up and angels of mercy brought Maman to her beloved son, Mishel, and also to Giti. The reunion was like another birth for Maman. Thankfully, the family members who fled Iran several years earlier graciously welcomed Maman without saying things like "we told you so."

After settling down in Israel, Maman carefully contacted her husband through phone calls to her two sons living in America, who then quietly and secretively passed on her messages through phone messages to Baba Nourie in Iran. He was warned to leave everything behind and get out since the Shah was about to give up his power to Muslim extremists, who now followed the soon-to-return exiled Ayatollah Khomeini. Baba Nourie listened to his wife's messages and promised he would join her at any cost.

After many long days of negotiating with human smugglers, Baba Nourie packed some clothing and other items for himself, Davood, and Lili. He also packed all his monetary savings in two suitcases, trusting that his smuggler friends would not suspect anything. He was wrong.

The escape was planned to include a great deal of traveling through Pakistan and stays in several villages along the way, to make sure the path was clear of Islamic Revolutionary Guards. After experiencing several hellish nights along the border, Baba Nourie, Davood, and Lili made it to Pakistan, but with no suitcases! The smugglers disappeared along with all their belongings and savings. Would God have mercy on this family again?

The three family members stayed at a site where a flood of refugees tightly crowded the rooms. Most of them were Iranian Jews. They were each waiting to take their turn flying out of Pakistan to Turkey and then applying for asylum in Israel.

Baba Nourie could hardly believe it when a Pakistani Jewish family came to visit him and his two grown children and asked them to stay in their home. The very kind Pakistani Jewish man even offered to make the very expensive phone calls overseas, making sure that Maman knew about her family's safety. So, Baba Nourie called his sons, Kamran and Moris, in America and asked them to purchase airline tickets for them to travel to Turkey and then to Israel.

In a matter of weeks, Baba Nourie, Davood, and Lili made it through the long, tedious days of waiting and eventually joined Maman and the rest of the family members in Israel. The promises of God never failed because of Maman's strong faith. The safe escape from Iran through dangerous borders, staying days and nights in several unknown border towns and villages, and meeting an amazing "angelic" Pakistani family could not have been possible without Maman's constant prayers. Even though Baba Nourie unfortunately lost all his cash savings hidden in his suitcases, he was thankful for his safety and for this unbelievable reunion. He often thought about his Iranian friends, Muslim or non-Muslim, who ended up losing their lives while fleeing Iran.

Tearfully, he held on to his weakened wife and kids and kissed them continuously. Most importantly he was thankful to God for the Promised Land, Israel, which He had promised to all the Jews many years ago. Their reliance on the promises of God carried the entire family through these difficult times.

CHAPTER SIXTEEN

AMERICA—GARAGE SALES AND BROKEN HEARTS

GITI HELPED THE FAMILY get situated in a nice town in Israel. The two-bedroom apartment, with a large living room connected to a modern kitchen, was more than enough space to accommodate everyone. Maman was thankful for all the blessings in Israel, but she missed her boys in America and wanted to see them soon since there were no travel restrictions between America and Israel. She called Kamran and Moris and asked if they would be willing to come to Israel, but since the boys had become American citizens and settled down, they suggested that Maman and Baba Nourie travel to America for a visit instead. The parents happily agreed. The boys arranged a non-stop flight from Israel to New York for

Maman and Baba Nourie.

Plans were made for Moris and his wife to drive from the state of Delaware, where they lived, to the JFK Airport in New York to help welcome their non-English speaking parents into the United States of America. It was a sweet reunion with Moris for Maman and Baba Nourie at the airport. They were especially delighted to meet their daughter-in-law, who had learned a little Farsi to communicate with them.

They all spent long hours together in various parts of New York. Maman was amazed by the multicultural mixes of people living together in the city. Baba Nourie talked about all the events that had happened during their escape and the new place where they now lived in Israel. Moris talked about his job in Delaware and explained that he was intently looking for a new job in Ohio in order to live near Kamran.

"You guys never told us details of how you met each other," Maman said to Moris and his wife.

"We were matched at our college by an Iranian Muslim couple!" Moris exclaimed happily.

"Isn't it interesting, Maman Joon, a Muslim couple introduced a Jew to a Christian and a happy marriage came out of this introduction!" Moris continued. They all laughed.

They had to stay at a hotel near the airport overnight to catch a flight to Ohio the next day to see Kamran.

Kamran was anxiously waiting for his parents' arrival. The Pelé-like soccer player could not wait to embrace Maman and show off his college degree!

"There's my soccer player boy," Maman screamed happily at the airport in Ohio. Baba Nourie was especially proud that his son settled down with a good-paying job. They all went to Kamran's house and enjoyed the reunion all day.

One of the best memories was that God blessed Moris with a new job only one week after Maman and Baba Nourie arrived in the States. So, instead of living more than a fourteen-hour drive away in Delaware, Moris and his wife were now only a two-hour drive away and weekly visits were enjoyed by all.

The happiest moment for Maman and her husband was the announcement of Moris' wife's pregnancy. The excitement of the news made Maman and Baba Nourie stay longer in America for the birth of their grandbaby. Baba Nourie could not help but tell his famous joke about pregnant women: "It's all a big giant gas in her belly!" They all laughed, even though Moris' wife had a puzzled look on her face at Baba Nourie's comment. Moris had to translate the comment quickly in order to avoid any language barrier conflict.

Maman and her husband stayed at Kamran's house the majority of the time since he was living by himself. Often they went to visit Moris and his wife and stayed for several days to help out, and Maman knit several colorful outfits for their new, soon-to-be-born grandbaby.

Baba Nourie remembered teasing Moris' wife when she was overdue by two weeks.

"I told you it was all gas; there is no baby in your belly!" Baba Nourie told Moris' wife. But he was wrong. Three days later Moris and his wife were blessed with a baby boy with long, black curly hair and dark brown eyes. It was a great moment for all.

Maman tried her best to be happy. She enjoyed cooking, knitting baby clothes, teaching her daughter-in-law the Persian language, and she even learned to speak a few necessary phrases in English. Her favorites were, "Ha var yoo [how are you]?", "You vant some tea?" and "Come on down," a popular saying from *The Price is Right* television game show. The best memories, however, were the garage sales during the heat of summer.

"Why do these Americans want to sell their nice things for a few pennies?" Maman asked with a big puzzled smile. But it was fun for her to collect items to make her home cozy. In her mind the concept of garage sales was as strange as the concept of Korsi is to Americans.

Despite all of the good memories, however, life in America was nothing like life in Iran or Israel. "America is a beautiful and God-blessed country, but life is too lonely here," Maman often mentioned to her boys. She was right, since one couldn't walk to the bazaar or shopping centers, but had to always ride in a car to go anywhere. Even though Kamran and Moris provided a great deal of comfort and happy memories, Maman's heart was still puzzled and wondered about a future with her distant family members. She missed her other children very much and longed to live near them once again.

After Maman and her husband had resided in Ohio for more than a year, Maman's breaking heart directed her, along with Baba Nourie, to return to Israel where Lili and Mishel clearly needed her company, as did Davood and Giti. Parting from Kamran, Moris, his wife and their grandbaby was very hard, but Maman's faith and trust in God spurred her on to The Promised Land. Maman and Baba Nourie traveled back to Israel with broken hearts, but with fun memories of many garage sale adventures.

CHAPTER SEVENTEEN
ISRAEL—THE FINAL HOME

THROUGH THE ISRAELI GOVERNMENT, Maman and Baba Nourie received financial assistance until they could move to a flat and live together with Davood, Lili, and Mishel. Several years passed, filled with joy and celebrations of High Holiday rituals, which were much more meaningful there than they had been in Iran.

Although Maman's heart always yearned for Iran, she was comforted by her children, grandchildren, and the Jewish culture all around her.

God never stopped blessing Maman during all her years of living in Israel. Lili lived with Maman and Baba Nourie for years. Lili poured out all her strength and soul to make sure her parents were comfortable. Giti was a great help with all the governmental paperwork, since she was very fluent in the Hebrew language and the customs in Israel. Life was so sweet. Maman was blessed with many grandchildren from Giti, Lili, and even her baby Mishel. More grandchildren also came into her life from her sons in America, including Davood who had also moved there. Maman and Baba Nourie traveled to America several times to visit Davood, Moris, and Kamran and their children. She was blessed for many years until diabetes began to take its toll.

Stress, Dialysis, and More

Mishel was drafted to serve in the Israeli Army for three years. The political situation in Israel was deteriorating with her neighboring Arab countries. The Israeli nation was always on high alert since there were many bus bombings and other terrorist activities inflicted on Israeli towns. The army had to be prepared for possible war at any moment, therefore all young boys and girls had to sign up for the army.

The news of Mishel joining the army brought back the awful memories of Mishel fleeing Iran alone. Even though

Mishel would be serving nearby, the thought of the terrorist attacks in Israel against army personnel and the possibility of Mishel going to war created high anxiety for Maman, which took a huge toll on her health. She started to experience tremendous stress, high blood pressure, depression, and worsening of her diabetes. Lili took Maman to many doctors to help her deal with these symptoms. Maman was put on many medications, but the stress of fleeing Iran and Mishel being in the army surrounded by terrorists was so traumatic that she had to be put on hemodialysis.

Lili, now married with two children, poured out all her strength and soul as she tended to Maman and kept a close eye on her many health problems. Lili was worried about Baba Nourie as well, since he had never fully recovered from the depression caused by losing all of his savings during their escape from Iran. Baba Nourie attended an Iranian synagogue most Friday evenings and Saturday mornings just to find some comfort. Although he was thankful to God for being safe after going through the hellish journey of fleeing Iran, losing his only dream house and all the savings, and most importantly watching his wife experience many health issues, became unbearable.

How much longer can a mother bear the stress of being worried about her children? What if our youngest son cannot make it through these nonsense terrorist attacks in Israel? How many trials are in God's will for Maman? Baba Nourie wondered. But Maman never gave up her faith in God and His wonderful promises. Constant prayers resulted in great news.

Mishel made it back safely from his three years of service in the Israeli Army, but one could see the load of depression and stress on his shoulders. He had to fake happiness for the sake of Maman's health. Seeing Maman undergo hemodialysis with the tangled, clear plastic tubes that carried fresh blood from one end of the machine to another, lasting for several hours every other day, was not easy for Mishel.

Maman remembered a day in the Hassan-Abad house when she showered Mishel with kisses and prayed at the same time to God to be alive to see his children someday. God did listen to her prayers and blessed Mishel and his wife with one boy and two girls.

The pain of dialysis shunts and needles in Maman's arms, the suffering from severe headaches from high blood pressure, and most importantly, being confined to a wheelchair due to the loss of strength in her knees, did not break her strong spirit and faith in God. When her sons visited her from America, she always reminded them to look up with a thankful heart and praise God for their lives. She did so with her fragile arms, which had many bruises from the dialysis injection sites, lifted up high in the air while repeating Khoda-Ra Shokert [Thank you, God].

Maman went through various types of treatments for her severe diabetes. Her kidney function kept failing to the point that the doctors recommended a kidney transplant. But Lili refused, since Maman's body was too weak to withstand the transplant operation. The doctors recommended continuing the hemodialysis, keeping a close watch on it, and trying other medications, so Maman had to stay in the hospital every other day for four hours of dialysis. Since Baba Nourie could not drive, Lili was the one who diligently took the necessary steps to make sure Maman would be taken care of in a timely manner.

The boys in America decided to visit Maman every year during summertime. The family reunions were short, but filled with many sweet memories for Maman. One of the memories Maman often recalled was when Moris stayed with her in the hospital during dialysis. Moris always carried his own Bible to read some passages to Maman while she was resting in bed.

"Do you know what Heaven looks like, Maman Joon?" Moris asked one day in the hospital, seated by her bed.

"I don't remember reading it in Torah," Maman replied with a tired voice.

"Well it's from the New Testament, you know, the forbidden book for the Jews," Moris replied cautiously.

"Well…it's God's word anyway," Maman replied. Moris smiled and started reading some verses from the last chapter of the Bible describing Heaven as a place with amazing pearly gates and beautiful precious stones and crystals. Most importantly, Heaven was the place where God resides who promised there would be no more tears or pain forever.

"This sounds great, Moris Joon, thank you," Maman replied. "I need to rest and sleep now."

Moris looked at Maman's face and smiled for several minutes, and then turned around to look at the dialysis machine with its many tubes attached to Maman's arms, with flowing blood circulating through filters and back into her veins.

There'll be no more pain, Maman Joon, Moris thought with joy.

There were several other dialysis patients in Maman's hospital room. Every time Maman was done with her dialysis, she would say goodbyes with a big smile to all the other dialysis patients around her.

"This is a great place where I feel a pure peace," Maman said to Moris on her way out of the hospital. "Several patients, doctors, and nurses are Arabs who are angels," Maman said. "I just wish those terrorists would pay a visit here before they decide to blow themselves up in a crowd," Maman continued sadly.

Maman's statement amazed Moris. He was very thankful to God for his mother, who had zero hate toward her enemy.

Many other good memories were made in Israel for several years. Maman's body was continually growing weaker every day, but she always sounded energetic and happy whenever she heard from her sons living in America, and she enjoyed watching her grandchildren and great-grandchildren grow up.

CHAPTER EIGHTEEN

FINAL PAIN

IT WAS THE HOT MONTH OF JUNE 2014 when Maman and Baba Nourie's grown children decided on another family reunion in Israel. This time, the sons in America, plus Kamran's daughter and grandson, traveled to Israel at the same time. Maman was in a great mood in spite of tremendous weakness from repeated dialysis for nearly eleven years. Her coughs were getting stronger and her breathing was more labored. Every time she had a health crisis, or when a combination of health issues popped up, everyone panicked, but her weak voice, repeatedly saying Ayb Nadareh [Persian for "It's not important"] gave everyone some comfort.

She had to use a walker to move around since her knees

were completely weakened and she had severe arthritis in all her toes.

"I wish God would give me back the strength to walk again," Maman sighed. But she never lost her will to move around and help Lili do some household chores. She could manage to push herself with her walker to the kitchen and lean over the sink to support her body against the edge of it to be able to wash the dishes. She also loved to chop the vegetables and clean the beef chunks to make her favorite dish, Ghormeh-Sabzi, but she needed help since her fingers were also weakened by the arthritis and by the bruises from the repeated dialysis injections. It used to take a long time to prepare this dish back in Iran, as she clearly remembered. It was hard to find Kosher meat, which was sold only by the few available Rabbis. When Maman or Baba Nourie found a Rabbi, they had to wait until the Rabbi said a prayer before butchering the sheep and cutting it into big chunks of meat to sell. Maman then had to clean the meat chunks thoroughly by getting rid of all the fat and veins, followed by cutting the meat into smaller chunks, washing and lastly salting them. All that labor just to prepare Kosher meat for a meal!

But here in Israel everything is Kosher. All meat prod-

ucts are pre-cleaned and pre-packaged and ready to cook, she thought. It was a blessing most Israelis didn't realize.

This time Maman could do a lot more chores than before, since she was energized by anxiously waiting for her American kids to visit.

"What time do they arrive?" Maman asked Lili.

"About a couple of hours or so, and good thing that today is the Sabbath so we can all enjoy a family reunion like we always had back in Iran," Lili replied.

Finally they heard a loud honking sound from outside the window. Maman reached out to the window and carefully leaned over to see her boys, Kamran's daughter and her son coming out of a taxi.

"Salam, Maman Joon, Salam!" screamed everyone outside while looking up to see Maman's head through the window.

"Ya-Allah, Ya-Allah [hurry up, hurry up] come on upstairs now," Maman yelled happily.

The boys left their luggage and raced upstairs, but were stopped by Mishel and Baba Nourie, who were waiting in the hallway to greet them. The joy of hugging and kissing Maman was incredible for the boys. As always, these yearly reunions rejuvenated Maman's spirit and gave her the physical strength for long hugs. Meeting Kamran's daughter and her son was another special delight for Maman.

During the two-week stay, everyone enjoyed spending more time with Maman and Baba Nourie. A visit to Jerusalem for an entire day was the most special event of all. At the Wailing Wall, men and women were praying in two separated fenced-in areas due to the Orthodox Jewish law. Giti and Lili took Maman, sitting in her wheelchair, to a small balcony overlooking the praying crowd. Maman covered her head with a long white scarf and stretched out her arms toward the Wall, praying with a thankful heart.

When the boys finished praying at the Wall, they turned around and were overjoyed to see Maman on the balcony, praying to God.

The sun is beaming through Maman's scarf on her head, making her look like an angel! Moris thought. This was an incredible day indeed. The voices of whispering prayers at the Wall, the loud Hebrew readings of the Torah by several teens celebrating their Bar-Mitzvah, and many people jotting down their personal prayers on small pieces of paper and inserting them into the holes of the Wall were unforgettable moments. Those pieces of paper with written personal notes symbolized direct prayer requests to God, according to the Jewish tradition.

The family spent the rest of the day touring several sightseeing places, and then headed home with many sweet memories. On the way home, Moris kept remembering Maman's face at the Wall and her joyful smiles. There was another special event that entered Moris' mind: one could hear the sound of the Hebrew prayers from several synagogues located in the alleys near the Wailing Wall, along with the sound of bells from some churches, and Muslim prayers from some nearby mosques, all at the same time! *It was a great day indeed*, Moris thought before he closed his eyes to nap.

On the last evening of the family reunion, Lili suggested a visit to the Kikar [a famous tourist area in Netanya where there are many shops, restaurants, and entertainment] to have pizza. Maman wore a warm, long, beautiful black jacket with a colorful scarf to cover her head. Baba Nourie showed great interest in staying up with everyone, even though it was long past his bedtime. At the Kikar, everyone was singing and dancing while fighting over the large olive-topped Israeli pizza. Baba Nourie felt like he was seventeen years old again, wanting a kiss from his bride, but Maman refused.

"We are too old for kissing each other!" Maman said, laughing, while turning her face away from her husband.

The final day of the family reunion arrived the next day. Maman had a silky white dress, which was a perfect match for her shiny white hair. She pushed her walker gently and made her way through the luggage laying on the floor to approach the door while waiting for her sweet goodbyes. She was in a great mood and happy to hear that her sons promised to return to Israel for a visit the next year. Everyone could feel the warm love radiating from her arms and kisses. The only thing they could not feel was the presence of angels surrounding Maman for her final departure from this earth and the great reunion with her firstborn son, Moris, in Heaven soon.

Moris approached Maman again for a final goodbye kiss and a photograph. While hugging each other, Moris whispered in Maman's ear, "Do you believe in Hashem and the Mashiah [Hebrew for Messiah], Yeshua?" Maman nodded yes.

Moris joyfully kissed Maman on her forehead, feeling delighted by Maman's response. *An assurance of her final home—Heaven,* he thought.

"I'll definitely come back next year, Maman Joon, perhaps with my own family too," Moris told Maman as he said the final goodbye to everyone. He kissed the Mezuzah on the exiting door and went downstairs.

As the airport taxi was slowly leaving Maman's house, the boys looked through the rear window of the taxi and saw Maman looking out from the third floor of the house, waving goodbye.

During the flight from Tel-Aviv to New York, Moris was constantly thinking of all the great memories he left behind in Israel, especially staying with Maman at the hospital during her dialysis and talking about God, Torah, and Heaven from the New Testament.

The plane touched down in New York in early morning, and after going through a lengthy process of immigration and security checks, there was about a two hour wait for the final flight to Ohio.

When everyone was in the boarding line, Moris received a phone call from Israel. He could hear crying and screaming in the background.

"Lili, is that you? What is going on?" Moris asked repeatedly.

Davood and Kamran looked at Moris worriedly and kept interrupting him for some explanation.

"Oh my God… Oh my God…" Lili repeatedly screamed with loud crying. "You must all turn around and come back immediately," she said, sobbing.

Moris gestured to his brothers to leave the boarding line and go to a quiet corner to talk. Moris gave the phone to Davood with a terrified look.

"Ok, Lili…calm down, stop crying for a minute and tell us what is going on," Davood said.

Lili tried to explain the situation while crying in a trembling voice.

"Maman collapsed after she was done with her dialysis and was rushed to intensive care," Lili explained.

Davood could clearly hear an awful screaming in the background, which told him the worst news.

"I need you guys to come back right now," Lili begged.

"We are just about to board our connecting flight to Ohio any minute. We cannot just buy tickets now and fly back to Israel. Let me talk to someone else now," Davood replied sternly.

Davood waited for several minutes while looking at the boarding line worriedly. Meanwhile, Moris and Kamran tried to explain to Kamran's daughter what was going on. Finally, Davood heard Giti's voice on the phone. She was fairly calm.

"It doesn't look good at all," Giti said. "Right now Maman is being treated at the ICU and the doctors are trying to figure out what happened."

"You guys fly home safely and call me when you arrive home," Giti continued.

Davood hung up the phone with a heavy heart and explained to everyone about Maman's situation. They all rushed to the boarding line to catch the next flight.

The two hour flight from New York to Ohio seemed long

and painful. Moris continuously prayed for Maman and the rest of the family in Israel. The thought of losing Maman was an excruciating one to bear.

Perhaps this is another emergency episode, like when Maman was rushed to the ER before, Moris thought. He remembered during one of his visits to Israel that Maman's blood pressure climbed so high she was rushed to the hospital. At her bedside, Moris had noticed Maman's anxiety attacks, confusion, severe chest pains and headaches. It was heartbreaking for Moris to watch. To his surprise, Lili had been unusually calm, since she had been through several ER episodes with several of Maman's health complications in the past. The heavy medications helped Maman to calm down and sleep all night. Amazingly, Maman had recovered quickly and had gone home the next day.

I pray that this is another similar ER experience for Maman and she'll be sent home tomorrow, Moris thought wishfully. But this time Lili wasn't calm at all, which scared Moris tremendously.

When they reached the Columbus airport, Davood called Giti to get an update.

"Unfortunately Maman went into a coma," Giti said with

a pained voice. She suggested that it would be better to contact her only, since Baba Nourie, Mishel and especially Lili were crying nonstop. Davood agreed.

The next day, Moris called Giti and insisted that he talk to one of the doctors in charge of Maman's care.

"Your mother had a severe brain stroke and is breathing through a ventilator," the doctor announced to Moris on the phone.

Moris informed his brothers that the likelihood of Maman surviving the stroke was not good at all, and suggested they look into booking a flight back to Israel soon.

The next day, June 10, 2014, Maman's soul was taken into God's presence.

The brothers mourned the loss of their mother together and shared their memories of Maman with thankful hearts. They were grateful to God for giving Maman eighty-two years of joyful life and the incredible love she had provided to all the children. Her endurance through years of harshness, poverty, homelessness, and above all the loss of her firstborn son in a tragic way, would be remembered forever. "Always look up and thank God for whatever you have in your life," was Maman's advice to all her children.

The brothers managed to travel back to Israel two days after returning home from there. They felt stunned throughout the flight and wished they could wake up at any moment to find that these tense days had all been a bad dream.

Lili and Mishel were waiting for their brothers' arrival at the Israeli airport. The reunion was a heartbreaking one. Lili looked like she had aged several years and Mishel started crying loudly while hitting his forehead with his hand. Davood tried hard to calm Mishel by hugging him and begging him to stop. They all comforted each other with long hugs and kisses.

When they arrived at the house, Davood, Moris, and Kamran broke down in tears as they looked up at the third-floor window and saw no one looking down greeting them. They could imagine Maman's head covered with her white scarf, smiling down at them. The crying intensified as soon as they all came inside the house and felt the absence of Maman. Lili had placed flowers, a tall enclosed candle in a clear, tall glass jar, and a couple of Maman's pictures around the couch where Maman used to rest. The brothers stared at Maman's pictures and continued crying for a while.

Everyone left the room except Moris. He sat down on the edge of Maman's bed facing the couch and stared at

Maman's pictures. While he was wiping away tears, he said a prayer quietly.

"I am so grateful to you, God, for your mercy and right timing that I could share the good news of Yeshua and your magnificent creation, Heaven, with my mother just several days before she passed away," Moris whispered. He then touched one of Maman's pictures and said: "Thank you, Maman, for all you did in our lives."

Baba Nourie was sitting on a corner of the couch in the living room, slouched with his head down, in obvious shock.

There were a couple of pictures of Maman on the end table next to the couch.

"He's been refusing to eat or to talk much," Lili told everyone. The brothers hugged their father and begged him to be strong since the one-week-long Jewish mourning period called Shiva would begin the next day. According to Shiva's rules, the siblings must remain home for seven days with no bathing, working, entertainment or cooking. They must pray by reading the Torah and remembering Maman's life. The relatives and neighbors brought food and started having evening-long prayers for the entire week.

Baba Nourie could only read a portion of Torah for a short time since he was weakened due to weight loss and lack of sleep. His walking ability worried Lili the most, since he had fallen several times coming from his bedroom to the living room. During the Shiva days, he was asked by his sisters and neighbors if he wanted to say something, anything, in memory of Maman.

"I just want my wife back, Hamsareh-Azizam [my dear wife]," he said repeatedly. The children kept reminding Baba Nourie that his wife had a good life and she could not live forever, but he seemed not to want to hear any comforting words from anyone.

The burial ceremony was filled with loud and sometimes deafening crying, especially when Maman's wrapped body was lowered into the grave. Baba Nourie sat on a small chair next to the grave and looked at his precious wife's body resting at the bottom. According to the Jewish burial ritual, everyone scooped some sandy soil by hand from the pile next to the grave and scattered it over Maman's body. The Hebrew prayer recited by a Rabbi at the graveside could hardly be heard since the crying was getting louder.

Mishel was the one who was crying the loudest and he screamed repeatedly, calling out to Maman Joon.

"It was all my fault, it was all my fault, I gave you all the stresses, I shortened your life, Maman Joon, since you were worried too much for me. Please forgive me, Maman Joon, please," Mishel cried out loud. Giti and Kamran were trying to calm Mishel by gently pouring cold water over his head and offering him water to drink. Mishel fell on the ground while continuing to sob. Davood rushed to Mishel's side and started washing his face to help him gain some strength.

Moris was putting flowers around the grave while continuously praying. He then picked up some small stones from around the grave and put them in his pocket to take home as keepsakes.

Lili was sitting on the ground close to Maman's grave, sobbing while placing colorful flowers all over the gravesite. Giti came and sat next to Lili for some comfort. They both wept bitterly.

The burial ceremony ended with each person laying down a flower on the grave while leaving the site. All the family members and relatives said their final goodbyes to a woman who left a legacy of great motherhood and strong faith in God.

The hot summer sun was beaming down on the graves in the cemetery, where there were various shaped tombstones decorated in the Hebrew, Farsi, Russian, and English languages. Some had engraved prayer verses from Torah next to the beautifully carved Star of David, and some had heart-warming sayings about the deceased person. Two rows away from Maman's grave there was a shiny black tombstone with an engraved Persian poem about an everlasting love between husband and wife.

While everyone was slowly walking away from the cemetery, Moris turned around and looked at Maman's grave. He pictured a beautiful reunion between Maman and her first son, Moris, in Heaven.

No more pain, Maman Joon, no more pain, he thought.

ABOUT THE AUTHOR
MORIS NIKNAM

Iranian-born, Moris K. Niknam, PhD, came to America thirty-nine years ago and received his master and doctoral degrees in chemistry. He is a US citizen, a proud Messianic Jew, married, and has four children. He is a full-time information chemist and a lecturer for religious and creation views. Currently he is writing a fictional novel as well as some self-faith and life-journey stories.

www.ingramcontent.com/pod-product-compliance
Lightning Source LLC
Chambersburg PA
CBHW051343040426
42453CB00007B/386